BY THE SAME AUTHOR

The Night Before Cookbook

FEASTS FOR TWO

FEASTS FOR TWO

A Cookbook of
Menus and Recipes for
Fifty Fabulous Meals

Paul Rubinstein

Macmillan Publishing Co., Inc.
New York

Macmillan Publishing Co., Inc.
Collier-Macmillan Canada Ltd.

Library of Congress Catalog Card Number: 72-92453

First Printing

Printed in the United States of America

Illustrations by Susan Obrant

For

JOY,

my love

Contents

Introduction

The concept of a dinner for two immediately brings to mind the idea of romance. Candlelight flickers over an intimate corner table enhanced by the soft glow of silver and the creamy richness of good linen. There is music adding to the atmosphere, a dusty bottle of vintage wine: everything is perfection!

This book is not about the staging and set decoration necessary to bring off such a feast and, of course, the inevitable social or marital triumph that follows. I leave all those decisions to the happy participants. This book is about how to prepare the food which will be served on that intimate table so that it *tastes* good.

When you are planning a dinner for two, the first and most constant problem you encounter is that of quantities. As anyone who has lived alone knows well, cooking in small quantities involves difficulties. But there are plenty of solutions. In the first place, food packaged in small amounts tends to be more expensive. This applies particularly to canned foods. On the other hand, for some reason known only to the manufacturers, frozen foods tend to be packaged in only one size, or designed so that you can remove part of the contents without the risk of thawing what's left. Therefore I have tried to use frozen instead of canned foods whenever possible.

Another difficulty lies with meats and fish. Here, of

course, it's easy to get precisely the right size of steak or the right number of lamb chops or shrimps. But the minute you're involved in standing rib roasts or poached whole fish, you may find it impossible to buy a reasonably small amount. There are two ways to deal with this problem, and I have used both in this book. One is to avoid it by simply never cooking these quantity-problem foods unless you have several guests. The other way is to use these foods but plan to include the remainder in a different recipe the next day or freeze and reheat it. If worse comes to worst, you can always get a household pet to clean up the leftovers!

Another difficulty is not having equipment of the proper size. If you are stuck with someone else's kitchen planning, everything may seem too big to cook your dinner for two. But the chances are that you're providing your own equipment, so there is plenty of choice. Nowadays, the variety of cooking utensils available is positively staggering. Most kitchenware manufacturers make pots and skillets and saucepans in a complete range of sizes. So take care and be sure to include the smallest sizes of the vital items when you stock your kitchen. In some cases, you are at an advantage when you cook for two. For instance, the usual electric blender jar is much too small to make soup for six or eight people and requires subdividing the ingredients and then running them through in separate batches. But that same jar is ideal for two! Small coffee pots are plentiful, and you can sometimes use a saucepan intended for some special purpose, such as melting butter, and make it perform perfectly as a regular pan for your own concoctions *à deux*.

Now that we have established that the important difficulties are quite manageable, here is how I have organized the recipes for easy use. Each section contains a different menu, ranging from picnics and lunches through dinners and late suppers. Naturally you can choose your main course and substitute dishes from other menus, but the ones given will serve as a guide from which to deviate.

Now all you have to do is find the right menu for your occasion, make a list of the ingredients, and head for the nearest grocery store. Good luck and happy dining for two!

Six Picnics for Two

—— ⚏——⚏——⚏——⚏——⚏——⚏——⚏——⚏——⚏——⚏——⚏——⚏——⚏——⚏——⚏——⚏——⚏——

PICNIC I

Cold Roast Beef and Mustard Sandwiches
on French Rolls

Cream Cheese, Radish, and Chive Dip

Corn Chips

Sliced Dilled Fresh Cucumber Salad

French Raspberry Jam Cookies

Iced Coffee

—— ⚏——⚏——⚏——⚏——⚏——⚏——⚏——⚏——⚏——⚏——⚏——⚏——⚏——⚏——⚏——⚏——

Cold Roast Beef and Mustard Sandwiches
on French Rolls

The most important thing is to make sure you get the best
French rolls—crisp and hard on the outside and fresh and
soft on the inside. Also, I recommend using very hot
English mustard in sparing amounts rather than gobs of
the usual mild varieties used in the United States.

4 French rolls
¼ lb. thinly sliced rare roast beef, fat trimmed away
hot English mustard
½ medium-sized onion
½ tsp. salt
¼ tsp. pepper
2 tbsp. butter

1. Slit the rolls in half and open, inner sides up, on a
sandwich board.
2. Spread butter thinly on the top of each half. Divide

3

the meat into four approximately equal amounts and lay it neatly on the bottom half of each roll.

3. Spread a very thin layer of the mustard on the meat and top that with paper-thin slices of onion. (These slices should be so thin that you can see through them.)

4. Sprinkle with salt and pepper. Close the sandwiches, slice them in half, diagonally, and secure each half with a toothpick. Wrap for your picnic basket.

Cream Cheese, Radish, and Chive Dip

1 8-oz. package cream cheese
3 tbsp. sour cream
6 radishes, peeled and finely chopped
2 tsp. finely chopped chives
1 tsp. lemon juice
½ tsp. seasoned salt
¼ tsp. white pepper
1 bag corn chips

1. In a bowl, soften the cream cheese, sour cream, and lemon juice together.

2. When softened, add the remaining ingredients (except the corn chips) and blend thoroughly.

3. Transfer to a sealable plastic container and refrigerate until packing in picnic basket.

Sliced Dilled Fresh Cucumber Salad

2 medium-sized cucumbers
½ cup white vinegar
2 tbsp. finely chopped fresh dill
½ tsp. salt
¼ tsp. freshly ground white pepper

4

1. Peel the cucumbers and slice thinly. Place in a small bowl or plastic container.
2. Mix together the remaining ingredients, pour over cucumbers, and let stand several hours or overnight. It is not necessary to refrigerate the cucumbers while they are soaking.
3. If you use a sealed plastic container, then simply transfer it to your picnic basket later.

French Raspberry Jam Cookies

These cookies are rich and delicious, but a bit fragile after they are baked. It is a good idea to use a tin box to transport them in, rather than relying on a plastic bag.

¼ lb. butter
1½ cups flour
¼ tsp. salt
¾ cup chopped almonds
¼ cup heavy cream
½ cup granulated sugar
1 cup raspberry jam or preserves

1. Take the butter out of the refrigerator and allow it to soften at room temperature. Sift the flour together with the salt and the sugar into a bowl.
2. Stir the almonds into the flour mixture, then add the softened butter and the cream. Knead thoroughly until all ingredients are well blended. Gather the dough into a ball and wrap it in waxed paper and refrigerate until it hardens.
3. While dough is chilling, preheat oven to 350 degrees and butter a cookie sheet.
4. Roll out the dough either on a pastry cloth or, even

better, on a marble slab. You will need two sizes of round cookie cutters, one with about half the diameter of the other. Now, with the larger of the cutters, cut out as many round cookies as possible. Then, with the smaller cutter, cut a circle out of the center of half the cookies. Transfer the cookies to the cookie sheet and bake for 8 to 9 minutes. Remove them from the sheet onto a rack to cool and harden.

5. When they are cool, spread the whole cookies with raspberry jam and top them with the cookie rings. Then add some more jam in the center to fill up the hole. You can reroll the dough from the centers you cut out and make a few more cookies in a second batch.

Iced Coffee

Make a quart of your favorite coffee, but make it about 50 percent stronger than you normally would for drinking it hot. Pour the coffee over a pitcher of ice cubes and refrigerate for at least an hour. Cool the inside of a Thermos by filling it with ice cubes and cold water and let it stand for about half an hour.

Add your preferred proportions of cream and sugar to the coffee and transfer to the Thermos, leaving out the ice cubes. Suggestion: if your guest likes cream and sugar while you prefer some different combination, use two small one-pint Thermoses instead of one big one. Don't forget to mark the outside so that you can tell them apart at the picnic.

§ NOTE: When packing any cold drink, it is a good idea to ice the inside of the Thermos with ice cubes and cold water, which should be discarded before pouring in the drink. This way your drink will remain cool and will not absorb heat from a Thermos which has been standing at room temperature.

PICNIC II

Fresh Liver Pâté

Thin Rye Bread Slices

Cold Steamed Half Lobster with Mustard-Mayonnaise

Mustard-Mayonnaise

Orange-Coconut-Banana Salad

Iced White Wine Punch

Fresh Liver Pâté

¼ cup finely chopped onions
3 tbsp. butter
¼ tsp. pepper
1 tsp. thyme
¼ tsp. salt
1 cup fresh whole chicken livers
6 oz. cream cheese

1. Sauté the onions in the butter over very low heat until softened, but do not allow them to brown. This should take 10 to 15 minutes. Add all the remaining ingredients except the cream cheese. Turn up heat and stir so that the livers get cooked on all sides for about 4 minutes.

2. Remove from heat and allow to cool for 15 minutes. Pass through a food mill or blender, add the cream cheese, and stir vigorously until well blended.

3. Pack the pâté into a crock or jar and refrigerate until ready to transfer to picnic basket.

Thin Rye Bread Slices

Have the man at your favorite delicatessen cut 6 or 8 slices of fresh rye bread into very thin slices on the meat cutting machine. Soften some butter, spread lightly on one side of each slice of bread, cut in half, wrap, and pack in picnic basket. Serve with the liver pâté.

Cold Steamed Half Lobster with Mustard-Mayonnaise

One-half lobster here is envisioned as a portion for one, so that you'll need to steam a whole lobster for two. If you are lobster lovers, however, you can double that and have a whole lobster per person. The directions

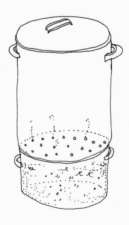

8

stay the same regardless. The essential equipment is either a big lobster steaming pot or any large pot with a steaming platform. The first of these is ideal and worth having for steaming many other things such as clams, corn, crabs, shrimps, and other foods. It is divided into two sections; the smaller, bottom part has a spigot to hold the boiling liquid which produces the steam, and the larger, top part has a perforated bottom to allow the steam to rise and cook the food inside. There is also a cover which fits on top of either section, depending on how you are using it. The alternative is a tall, large stock pot in which you place a steaming platform to prevent the food from being immersed in the water. It is a bit less comfortable to use, but produces the same results.

> 1 *live 2-lb. lobster.*
> 1 *bay leaf*
> 2 *cloves garlic, cut into several pieces*
> 1 *tbsp. vinegar*
> 2 *tbsp. olive oil*

1. Fill the lower part of your steamer ¾ full of water and add the bay leaf, garlic, vinegar, and oil. Bring to a boil.
2. When the water is boiling, and you can see steam rising briskly through the holes in the perforated bottom of the top part of the steamer or up through the holes in the steaming platform, drop in the live lobster and cover immediately.
3. Allow it to steam for about 20 minutes. Remove lobster from pot and chill in the refrigerator.
4. When the lobster is cold, place it on its back on a wooden cutting board and split it down the middle

with a large chef's knife or cleaver. If you use a cleaver you can also split the large sections of the claws with it, or else use a lobster cracker.

5. Wrap the half-lobsters in aluminum foil and place in picnic basket.

Mustard-Mayonnaise

The proportions and the strength of mustard you use should be arrived at through trial and error, since everyone has his own level of tolerance for strong sauces. The ingredients given below produce a relatively mild strength.

1 cup mayonnaise
1 tbsp. prepared Dijon or English mustard
1 tsp. lemon juice
1 dash Worcestershire sauce
¼ tsp. freshly ground pepper

1. Vigorously stir all the ingredients together in a bowl.
2. Pack in a sealed plastic container and keep refrigerated until transfer to picnic basket.

Orange-Coconut-Banana Salad

1 fresh whole coconut
3 large navel oranges
3 large bananas
1 cup fresh orange juice
½ cup sugar
2 tbsp. kirsch

1. Split the coconut open, discard (or save) the juice, strip the white meat from the inside of the shell. Run

it through a food mill equipped with a coarse blade, or grate using a coarse grater.

2. Cut the rind, including the bitter white inner skin, away from the oranges, then cut into sections. Carefully remove seeds and skins between the sections. This is easy to do with a very sharp paring knife.

3. Peel and slice the bananas into ¼-inch slices.

4. Put all the fruit into a bowl, add the orange juice, sugar, and kirsch, and toss lightly. Refrigerate for several hours. Toss occasionally.

5. Pack in a plastic container for transfer to picnic basket.

Iced White Wine Punch

1 bottle of your favorite dry white wine
1 thinly sliced lemon
2 tbsp. sugar
2 dashes orange bitters
2 jiggers vodka

1. Partially fill a large pitcher with ice cubes.

2. Combine all the ingredients in the pitcher, stir to make sure the sugar dissolves, and refrigerate for at least one hour.

3. Transfer punch to a large Thermos bottle, leaving out the ice cubes, and pack in picnic basket.

PICNIC III

Caviar and Cream Cheese Sandwiches
Smoked Salmon Sandwiches
Westphalian Ham Sandwiches
Tomatoes with Roquefort Stuffing
Hard-Cooked Eggs with Mayonnaise Dip
Fresh Brandied Peaches
Iced Mint Tea

Caviar and Cream Cheese Sandwiches

*1 4-oz. jar red caviar (You may use black beluga caviar
if you can afford it!)*
1 cup sour cream
8 thin slices white sandwich bread, crusts trimmed off
1 tsp. lemon juice
¼ tsp. white pepper
8 radishes, peeled and chopped

1. Combine the sour cream, lemon juice, pepper, and radishes and mix well.
2. Then gently stir in the caviar, taking care not to crush the eggs.
3. Lay out half the bread slices on a board and spread them as evenly as possible with the mixture.
4. Cover with remaining slices of bread, then cut each sandwich diagonally in half and secure each half with a toothpick.

5. Wrap the sandwiches individually in plastic film and refrigerate until transfer to picnic basket.

Smoked Salmon Sandwiches

¼ lb. thinly sliced smoked Nova Scotia or Scotch salmon
8 thin slices Scandinavian pumpernickel bread
1 lemon, quartered
1 pepper mill containing fresh black peppercorns

1. Lay out half the slices of pumpernickel.
2. Carefully cover each slice with the salmon, trimming the salmon slices to fit.
3. Squeeze a little lemon juice over each sandwich. Grind pepper over sandwiches (about one turn of the pepper mill over each).
4. Top the sandwiches with the rest of the bread slices, cut diagonally in half and wrap in plastic film. Refrigerate until ready to transfer to picnic basket.

Westphalian Ham Sandwiches

For those who don't know, Westphalian ham is similar to Italian prosciutto, but the texture is more firm, and it tends to be a little more salty. The smoky flavor is more pronounced. Because of its hardness, the ham can be sliced extremely thin without danger of tearing—and I recommend the thinnest possible slices. Warning: If you have sliced it too thick, it will be difficult to bite through the sandwich.

¼ lb. thinly sliced Westphalian ham
¼ cup radishes, peeled and finely chopped
½ cup soft cream cheese
½ tsp. black pepper
8 very thin slices fresh rye bread

1. Lay out four slices of the bread on a board.
2. Mix cream cheese, radishes, and pepper thoroughly.
3. Spread a thin layer of the cream cheese mixture on each of the four slices of bread. Then divide the ham into four equal portions and arrange it neatly on top of the cream cheese.
4. Top the ham with more of the cream cheese mixture.
5. Cover the sandwiches with the other four slices of bread. Trim away any ham hanging out the sides, slice each sandwich in half, and wrap in plastic film for the picnic basket.

Tomatoes with Roquefort Stuffing

> 2 *medium-to-large firm ripe tomatoes*
> 2 *tbsp. crumbled Roquefort (or equivalent) cheese*
> 1 *tbsp. finely minced fresh celery*
> 1 *tsp. mayonnaise*
> ⅛ *tsp. salt*
> ⅛ *tsp. pepper*

1. Cut a ¼-inch slice from the top of each tomato and set aside.
2. With a teaspoon, scoop out about half the meat from the inside of the tomatoes and place pulp in a bowl.
3. Add the remaining ingredients to the pulp and blend thoroughly.
4. Stuff the tomatoes with the mixture, taking care not to tear the skin.
5. Cap the stuffed tomatoes with the top slices of the tomatoes. Refrigerate until ready to pack for the picnic basket.

Hard-Cooked Eggs with Mayonnaise Dip

6 eggs
¾ cup mayonnaise
1 tsp. hot English mustard
2 tsp. lemon juice
¼ tsp. Lawry's Seasoned Salt

1. Hard-cook the eggs and remove them from the water. Allow them to cool, then peel and wrap them in plastic film for the picnic basket.
2. Mix the remaining ingredients together thoroughly and pack in container to accompany eggs as a dip.

Fresh Brandied Peaches

These don't taste like the brandied peaches you can buy in an adorable wooden keg for an astronomical price at your local gourmet shoppe! They taste like fresh peaches and should be served ice-cold, if possible, and with a delicious hint of brandy.

4 to 6 fresh just-ripe peaches
½ cup good brandy or cognac
2 dashes orange bitters
½ cup sugar
¼ cup lemon juice

1. Very carefully peel and pit the peaches, then cut in quarters or eighths, depending on the size of the fruit. Pack slices tightly in a bowl.
2. Mix the brandy, bitters, sugar, and lemon juice together in a separate bowl and stir until the sugar is dissolved.
3. Pour the resulting syrupy liquid over the peaches,

making sure all the slices are covered. If they are not, use a different-shaped bowl, or add a little more brandy.
4. Let stand at least overnight without disturbing before packing in picnic basket.

Iced Mint Tea

1 qt. strong tea
1 thinly sliced orange
2 tbsp. sugar (more, if you like)
3 sprigs fresh mint
2 tbsp. lemon juice

NOTE: When brewing the tea, whether you use tea bags or loose tea, add the fresh mint leaves to the hot water at the same time as you add the tea.
1. Ice a Thermos with cold water and ice cubes. Discard the contents just before pouring in the tea.
2. Partially fill a large pitcher with ice cubes.
3. Mix the mint tea with the remaining ingredients, stir well, and pour over the ice cubes into the pitcher.
4. Let stand in the refrigerator at least one hour, then transfer to the cold Thermos, leaving out the ice cubes.

—||—||—||—||—||—||—||—||—||—||—||—||—||—||—||—||—||—||—||—||—||—||—

PICNIC IV

Selection of Danish Open-Face Sandwiches
on Scandinavian Rye
Fresh Fruit Salad
Mocha Chip Cookies
Iced Rum Punch

—||—||—||—||—||—||—||—||—||—||—||—||—||—||—||—||—||—||—||—||—||—||—

Selection of Danish Open-Face Sandwiches
on Scandinavian Rye

Here we have a selection of six different kinds of sandwiches, two of each. The best way to approach preparing
and packing them for your picnic is to start with a
square of plastic film, flat on the sandwich board, then
put the slice of bread on top of it. After you have added
all the ingredients, you can wrap the sandwich, gathering
the plastic film to seal, and making a little cushion
over the top. This will avoid spills and make the sandwiches attractive, as well as intact, when they are un-
wrapped.

*12 thin slices of Scandinavian rye bread (or domestic,
if necessary)*

Danish Ham and Cream Cheese

2 oz. cream cheese
4 slices pink Danish cooked ham

Spread two slices of bread with 1 oz. cream cheese. Top
each with two slices of ham, trim edges, wrap, and pack.

Chopped Herring and Onion

2 very thin slices fresh onion
½ cup chopped herring
1 tbsp. softened butter

Spread two slices of bread with softened butter. Then cover each with half the chopped herring, top with thin onion slices, and wrap.

Smoked Salmon and Egg

1 sliced hard-cooked egg
1 tsp. lemon juice
¼ tsp. black pepper
1 tbsp. softened butter
2 thin slices smoked salmon (about ⅛ lb.)

Spread two slices of bread with the butter. Then carefully cover with thin slices of hard-cooked egg, without breaking the slices. Now fit one slice of the salmon on each piece, sprinkle with lemon juice and black pepper, and wrap.

Maatjes Herring and Dill with Mustard Sauce

1 small can Maatjes herring fillets
1 tbsp. freshly chopped dill
1 tbsp. mayonnaise
½ tsp. hot English mustard

Mix the mayonnaise, mustard, and half the dill together in a small bowl. Spread two slices of bread with the mixture, then carefully lay out the herring fillets on top. Sprinkle with the remaining fresh dill, and wrap.

Shrimps and Pink Mayonnaise

4 cooked jumbo shrimps
1 tbsp. mayonnaise
½ tsp. tomato paste
½ tsp. lemon juice
1 tsp. chopped parsley

In a small bowl, mix the mayonnaise, lemon juice, and tomato paste. Spread both slices of bread with the mixture. Slice the shrimps in half lengthwise. Arrange four shrimp halves on each piece, sprinkle with parsley, and wrap.

Tartar Steak

½ cup freshly ground round steak
½ tsp. Worcestershire sauce
1 tbsp. finely chopped onion
1 anchovy fillet
1 raw egg yolk
½ tsp. fresh black pepper

Mix all the ingredients thoroughly in a bowl, using two forks. Spread two slices of bread with the mixture, then wrap.

Fresh Fruit Salad

This recipe should be prepared in advance, if possible. Although I give a specific list of fruits to be used, almost any substitute is acceptable as long as balance is maintained between the more acid fruits (such as citrus fruits or pineapple) and the sweeter ones (melons, pears, etc.).

2 firm but ripe pears, peeled and cored
1 large apple, peeled and cored
1 grapefruit, sectioned, pitted, and peeled
1 banana, peeled and sliced
1 small cantaloupe, cut into balls
1 cup seedless grapes
1 cup strawberries, husked, washed, and cut in half
½ cup granulated sugar
2 tbsp. kirsch or other fruit liqueur

1. Slice or cut into a bowl all the fruit into bite-size pieces (except the grapes). Cut the grapes in half lengthwise and add.
2. Sprinkle with granulated sugar and toss gently to mix the fruit.
3. Sprinkle the kirsch over the top and allow to stand in the refrigerator overnight, or at least a few hours. If there are any foods with pronounced odors (such as cheese or salami) in the refrigerator, cover top of the fruit bowl with plastic film.
4. Just before packing for the picnic, transfer the fruit salad to plastic container, seal, and pack.

Mocha Chip Cookies

½ cup brown sugar
½ cup butter
1 egg, beaten
½ tsp. baking soda
2 tsp. very strong coffee
1 cup flour, sifted
6 oz. chocolate chips
½ cup chopped almonds

1. Allow the butter to soften and stir the sugar into it until well blended.
2. Add the remaining ingredients and mix well.
3. Preheat oven to 350 degrees. Butter and lightly flour a cookie sheet.
4. Drop dough, one tablespoon at a time, onto cookie sheet, leaving plenty of room between cookies. (Drop the first cookie and see how far it spreads out before doing the next one.)
5. Bake the cookies for 10 or 11 minutes, then remove from oven and slip them onto a cooling rack.
6. Pack the finished cookies in a tin box for transfer to the picnic basket.

Iced Rum Punch

1 cup Myers's dark rum
1 cup pineapple juice
3 dashes orange bitters
2 tbsp. sugar
2 tsp. lemon juice
1 8-oz. bottle ginger ale

1. Combine all the ingredients in a pitcher and refrigerate until almost ready to pack for the picnic.
2. Just before transferring to Thermos, fill pitcher to top with cracked ice and stir. Then strain out ice, pour into Thermos, and close tightly.

PICNIC V

Cold Fresh Salmon with Green Mayonnaise
Sliced Tomato and Onion Salad
Buttered Hard Rolls
Half Cantaloupes with Lime
Iced Chablis

Cold Fresh Salmon with Green Mayonnaise

1½-lb. piece fresh salmon
1 pt. clam juice
2 carrots, peeled
2 stalks celery
1 cup finely chopped onion
2 tbsp. butter
½ tsp. freshly ground white pepper
½ cup white wine

1. Put butter into belly opening of salmon and place in a covered saucepan or stew pot. Surround with the chopped onions, carrots and celery and sprinkle with pepper.
2. Add the clam juice and wine, cover, and poach over medium heat for about 20 minutes. The salmon is ready when the pale pink cooked color extends to its thickest part, but the meat is still firm.
3. Remove carefully from the cooking liquid, using two slotted spoons or a spatula and a spoon to avoid breaking

the fish. Pack in plastic container for your picnic basket.
Serve with green mayonnaise dressing.

GREEN MAYONNAISE

1 cup mayonnaise
1 tsp. lemon juice
1 dash Worcestershire sauce
1 tbsp. chopped parsley
½ tsp. Lawry's Seasoned Salt
¼ tsp. freshly ground white pepper
4 drops green vegetable food coloring

Briskly mix all the ingredients together in a mixing bowl.
Transfer to a container for the picnic basket and refrigerate until last minute.

Sliced Tomato and Onion Salad

2 medium-sized beefsteak tomatoes
2 medium-sized Bermuda onions
½ cup wine vinegar
¼ tsp. freshly ground pepper
¼ cup olive oil
¼ tsp. salt
1 tbsp. chopped parsley
1 tsp. chopped chives

1. Peel and slice the onions into thin slices. Put the onion
slices into a bowl and cover with the wine vinegar and
pepper. Allow to soak for about two hours.
2. Remove the onion slices and set aside. Save about half
of the remaining liquid. Add the olive oil, salt, parsley,
and chives to the liquid and mix thoroughly and use as
a dressing.

3. Slice the tomatoes and toss with the onion slices in the dressing. Pack into a container for your picnic basket.

§ NOTE: It is particularly appealing to peel the tomatoes before slicing, but of course this step is optional. To peel tomatoes, lodge the tomato securely on the end of a long-handled two-tine fork. Turn on the flame of a gas burner, and slowly rotate the tomato over the flame. When you notice the red skin turning slightly yellow and then splitting in one or two places, remove from heat. Using a small, sharp paring knife, the skin should come off smoothly in only one or two pieces.

Buttered Hard Rolls

1 tbsp. softened butter
2 fresh hard rolls

Cut the hard rolls in half horizontally. Butter both inside surfaces, put back together like a sandwich, and wrap in plastic film. Refrigerate to keep fresh until time to transfer to picnic basket.

Half Cantaloupes with Lime

1 ripe but firm cantaloupe
1 large fresh lime
½ cup granulated sugar

1. Cut the cantaloupe in half and scoop out the central pulp and seeds.
2. Place half the sugar in each half melon.
3. Cut the lime into four quarters and pack two quarters, skinside down, in each half cantaloupe. Now wrap each half melon with plastic film and refrigerate until ready to add to the picnic basket.

4. When serving, remove lime wedges and squeeze their juice into the center of the melon to mix with the sugar. This creates a delightful accent to the taste of the melon.

PICNIC VI

Vodka Watermelon
Cold Roast Squab
Potato Salad
Assorted Cheese
Chocolate Brownies
Iced Tea

Vodka Watermelon

This idea is not new, but I've never seen it in a cookbook and it is too good to miss for a picnic. Make sure the person who has to drive home afterwards doesn't get more than his share of it!

1 small watermelon
1 pt. vodka

1. Cut two plugs about the size and shape of wine corks out of the rind at opposite ends of the watermelon.
2. Stand the watermelon on end in your kitchen sink, with the hole at the bottom over the drain opening.
3. Forget about it for a few hours, until most of the "water" has drained out of the melon. If you want to be accurate, you can set the watermelon up to drain with a

receptacle to catch the "water." This way you can measure how much vodka it will absorb.

4. When drained, tightly replace one of the two plugs.

5. Fill the watermelon with vodka by pouring it carefully into the other hole. This can be done either with a funnel, or by shoving the neck of the bottle firmly into the hole and holding it up until the bottle is empty.

6. Now replace the other plug, and put the watermelon in the freezer overnight to freeze the melon. Remember, the vodka inside won't freeze because it is almost pure alcohol and would require temperatures much lower than your freezer is capable of producing.

7. When leaving on your picnic, take the watermelon along. It will start to thaw out, but will remain nice and cold on the inside.

8. There are two ways to serve the watermelon. One is simply to slice it and eat it as though it hadn't been doctored up! The other way is to punch holes in it large enough to insert ordinary drinking straws and slowly drink the vodka.

Cold Roast Squab

2 fresh squabs, cleaned and ready for roasting
1 10½-oz. can chicken broth
¼ lb. butter
2 strips bacon
1 tbsp. poultry seasoning
1 tsp. salt

1. Preheat oven to 325 degrees.

2. Dry squabs inside and out with a paper towel.

3. Salt the insides of the squabs. Soften some of the butter and spread it over the outer skins of the squabs.

Then divide the bacon strips in half and lay one half on each side of the breastbone of each squab. Sprinkle squabs with poultry seasoning, then place on a rack in a roasting pan, and bake for 20 minutes per pound.

4. As soon as you have put the squabs in the oven, put the chicken broth into a small saucepan over low heat. Add the neck, giblets, and livers of the squabs and the rest of the butter. This will be your basting liquid.

5. Keep an eye on the squabs as they cook. (A glass-door oven is ideal for this so that you don't have to continually open the door and let the heat escape.) Every time the skin begins to look a little dry or bubbles of air form under the skin, baste with some of the liquid from the saucepan mixed with the drippings in the bottom of the roasting pan. The implement easiest to use for this is a bulb baster—well worth buying if you don't own one.

6. The squabs are done when the skin is golden brown, and the drippings from the birds have diminished.

7. Remove the birds from the oven and set aside to cool. When cooled, wrap each squab tightly in aluminum foil and transfer to the refrigerator to await packing in the picnic basket. You may retain the basting liquid, if any is left, for future use, or discard.

Potato Salad

3 large mature potatoes, peeled
2 hard-cooked eggs, chopped
1 stalk finely chopped celery
½ cup finely chopped onion
1 tsp. salt
¼ tsp. white pepper
¾ cup mayonnaise

1. Boil the potatoes in slightly salted water for about 12 minutes or until cooked through but still firm. Remove from water and set aside to cool.
2. Combine the remaining ingredients in a bowl and mix well.
3. Dice the cooled potatoes into about ½-inch cubes.
4. Add the potatoes to the other mixture and mix again, making sure the potato cubes are coated with the mayonnaise.
5. Pack in a plastic container and refrigerate until ready to transfer to the picnic basket.

Assorted Cheese

The trick here is to *buy* correctly. Hopefully, you have a good cheese shop available to you or, at least, a good delicatessen counter which stocks fine cheeses. As far as supply is concerned, there are no cheeses in this modern age of refrigeration which are seasonal. There have been entire books written on the subject of cheese, and I am not attempting to cover the subject here. Pick a good selection of three or four cheeses, such as a brie, a Danish blue, and a Gruyère. Or use one of the soft cheeses, like a Boursin, or a Crema Danica. Remember, if you buy too much, cheeses can always be used up at a later date in salad dressings, omelettes, or for hors-d'oeuvres.

Chocolate Brownies

2 *oz. unsweetened cooking chocolate (If you use high-quality Swiss chocolate which contains some sugar, simply reduce the sugar in this recipe by about 2 tbsp.)*
1 *cup granulated sugar*
½ *lb. butter*
2 *eggs*
1 *cup flour, sifted before measuring*
2 *tsp. coffee syrup or very strong coffee*
1 *cup chopped almonds or walnuts*

1. In a double boiler, melt the chocolate, butter, and sugar together over simmering water. Stir continuously until melted and smoothly combined, then remove from heat. Preheat oven to 350 degrees.
2. In a separate bowl, beat the eggs. Stir the chocolate mixture into the beaten eggs and mix thoroughly.
3. Add the remaining ingredients and mix thoroughly again.
4. Butter the bottom and sides of a 6-inch × 10-inch pan. Pour the mixture into the pan and bake for about 20 minutes in the preheated oven.
5. When ready, remove pan from oven and cut the brownies in the pan into squares or rectangles with a sharp knife. Leave in pan and allow to cool.
6. To pack for picnic, carefully remove brownies with a flexible spatula and wrap individually in plastic film.

Ten
Lunches for
Two

LUNCH I

Omelette with Sour Cream and Red Caviar
Tossed Green Salad, Chive Dressing
Thin Rye Toast
Lemon Sherbet
Citrus Vodka Punch

Omelette with Sour Cream and Red Caviar

The most crucial decision to make here is the number of eggs in the omelette. This is ruled by the size of your omelette pan. The ideal 3-egg omelette should be prepared in an omelette pan which is about 9 inches in diameter. The best pans are made of heavy-gauge aluminum, never used for anything else but omelettes and, above all, never washed. They should be simply wiped with a fistful of paper towels after each use. A 2-egg omelette should be made in a 7-inch pan, and a 4-egg omelette in a 10- or 11-inch pan. Don't try to use more than 4 eggs in an omelette. I give here the 3-egg omelette recipe which can be added to, or subtracted from, by a one-third proportion for the other sizes.

3 eggs
1 tbsp. butter
½ pt. sour cream
1 2-oz. jar red caviar
¼ tsp. salt
1 tbsp. cold water

§ NOTE: These ingredients are for ONE omelette. Double them for TWO.

1. Put two dinner plates in the warming oven before you start.

2. Beat the eggs, water, and salt together with a fork or wire whisk and place conveniently near the stove.

3. Open the container of sour cream and put it, along with a large spoon, near the beaten eggs. Open the container of red caviar and place it, along with a small spoon, near the eggs.

4. Heat the omelette pan over high heat until a drop of water dropped on the surface sizzles and rolls around quickly without breaking up. Then reduce heat to medium low.

§ NOTE: Before you begin making the omelette, it is important to know that the whole process only takes about 2 minutes from beginning to end. Therefore, everything you need must be within reach, and you must be prepared to move quickly. One additional implement needed is a long, straight, flexible-bladed spatula.

5. Take out one warm plate. Toss the butter into the hot pan. *Immediately* pour in the beaten eggs. Stir the eggs around the pan briskly with the fork. At the same time, occasionally give the pan a good shake (back and forth motion) to make sure the omelette doesn't stick. When the eggs begin to set (harden a bit on the bottom) but remain runny and loose on top, add half the sour cream and half the caviar. Spread the caviar and sour cream as evenly as possible over the omelette. Remember, this must be done quickly or the bottom will get overdone. Now tip the pan away from you and, as you tip it, slip the spatula under the edge nearest you and fold it over,

very gently. (After the omelette is completely folded over, if the bottom you have just exposed doesn't look done enough, let it cook a few seconds longer in the tipped-up pan.)

6. To transfer the omelette to the plate, simply place the tipped edge of the pan at the edge of the plate and turn the pan completely upside down over the plate, reversing the omelette. This also will conceal any leakage or ragged edges. Garnish the omelette with the remaining sour cream along one side and the red caviar on the other. Top with a few grains of the caviar and serve immediately. You can add a sprig of parsley for color if you wish.

§ NOTE: This technique for making an omelette should be practised a couple of times at home alone—with no distractions—before trying it with a guest present!

Tossed Green Salad, Chive Dressing

1 small head bib lettuce
1 head endive
1 small bunch watercress
3 tbsp. olive oil
1 tbsp. lemon juice
¼ tsp. salt
¼ tsp. white pepper
1 tbsp. freshly chopped chives

1. Wash the lettuce, endive, and watercress. Separate the leaves of the lettuce and endive and tear them into pieces no larger than approximately 1½ inches square. Cut the thick stems away from the watercress leaves and discard.
2. Drain the leaves in a colander.
3. Blend the remaining ingredients thoroughly in the bottom of a wooden salad bowl and leave until serving.
4. To serve, put the drained salad into the bowl containing the dressing and toss until the leaves are well coated with the dressing.

Thin Rye Toast

There is a trick to doing this. You must use either the broiler in your stove or the type of electric toaster that is also designed to operate as a small warming oven, in which the food is exposed horizontally to the heating elements rather than vertically as in the typical two-slot toaster.

8 paper-thin slices rye bread (preferably sliced at the delicatessen on the meat slicing machine)
2 tbsp. very soft butter

1. Lay the bread on a board, and spread evenly with a

thin layer of butter. Don't allow any lumps of butter to remain.

2. Put into the broiler as many slices of the bread as the size of your broiler or toaster allows. The heat should be *above* the bread, and there should be a solid catch-tray underneath to catch any butter that drips down.

3. Watch carefully as the bread toasts. It is ready when the slices curl a bit and become rigid, and the edges closest to the heat start to char. Remove quickly from heat, place in a basket lined with a napkin, fold napkin over the toast to retain heat, and serve immediately with the omelette.

Lemon Sherbet

1 tsp. unflavored gelatin
½ cup sugar
1 tsp. grated lemon rind
½ cup lemon juice
1 egg white

1. Dissolve the gelatin in 4 tbsp. lukewarm water until every grain has disappeared.

2. In an enameled saucepan, boil 1½ cups of water with the sugar for about 10 minutes until a syrup begins to form. Then add the dissolved gelatin to the syrup, stir well, remove from heat and place the pan in the refrigerator to chill.

3. When chilled, mix the grated lemon rind into the lemon juice and stir the mixture into the syrup.

4. In a separate bowl, beat the egg white until stiff. Fold the beaten egg white into the lemon syrup mixture.

5. Place the mixture into a mold, or any suitable con-

tainer. (A metal container is best because it conducts the cold better.) Put the container in your freezer.

6. When the sherbet begins to freeze and get slushy, stir it well in order to break down the larger crystals. Return it to the freezer. This procedure should be carried out at least twice during the freezing process.

7. To serve, unmold sherbet onto serving dish or, if you have used individual molds, onto individual dessert plates.

Citrus Vodka Punch

1 cup vodka
½ cup orange juice
½ cup lemon juice
1 sliced orange
1 sliced lemon
½ cup granulated sugar
3 dashes orange bitters

Mix all the ingredients together in a pitcher with ice cubes. Serve very cold.

LUNCH II

Vichyssoise
Chef's Salad, Louis Dressing
Pommes à l'Huile
Fresh Raspberry Gelatin
Iced Brandied Coffee

Vichyssoise

2 medium-sized potatoes
6 leeks, about ½ inch in diameter
1½ pts. chicken broth
1 tsp. salt
¼ tsp. white pepper
½ cup heavy cream
1 tbsp. minced fresh chives

1. Peel the potatoes and slice into ⅛-inch slices. Mince the white parts of the leeks very finely.

2. Simmer the potatoes and leeks in the chicken broth for about 30 minutes or until very tender. Then run the mixture through a blender or through a food mill followed by a very fine sieve.

3. Add the cream and the seasonings and stir. Chill in refrigerator.

4. Serve ice cold, in chilled soup cups. Just before serving,

sprinkle half the minced fresh chives on the surface of the soup in each cup. It is very important that these chives be fresh.

Chef's Salad, Louis Dressing

1 small head bib lettuce
1 large ripe tomato
4 slices boiled ham
4 slices Swiss cheese
8 black olives
4 slices smoked turkey
4 hard-cooked eggs

1. Wash, tear the lettuce, and place in colander to drain.
2. Cut the ham, cheese, and turkey into long thin strips about ¼-inch wide.
3. Cut the tomato into 8 wedges.
4. Peel and cut the 4 hard-cooked eggs into quarters.
5. When the lettuce is drained, arrange it as a bed in your salad bowl. Then arrange, in an attractive pattern, the tomato, egg wedges, and the strips of ham, turkey and cheese, punctuating with the black olives. Bring the

dressing to the table in a separate dish. When ready to serve, spoon the dressing over the salad and toss.

LOUIS DRESSING

1 cup mayonnaise
¼ cup chili sauce
1 tsp. horseradish
2 tsp. Worcestershire sauce
½ tsp. Lawry's Seasoned Salt
¼ tsp. freshly ground pepper
1 hard-cooked egg

1. Peel and force the hard-cooked egg through a sieve into a mixing bowl.
2. Add all the other ingredients and mix briskly. Serve with the salad.

Pommes à l'Huile

3 medium-sized potatoes
4 strips bacon, cooked crisp and crumbled
1 tbsp. olive oil
½ tsp. salt

1. Peel and cook the potatoes in rapidly boiling salted water until a fork easily goes into one.
2. Remove the potatoes from the water and drain. Allow them to cool to room temperature.
3. Cut the potatoes into roughly ½-inch cubes. Sprinkle them with salt and crumbled bacon. Pour the oil over the salad and toss lightly to coat the potatoes with the oil.
4. Cover salad bowl with plastic film and keep at room temperature until ready to serve.

Fresh Raspberry Gelatin

Don't worry if fresh raspberries are out of season. This dessert comes out just as well using frozen ones. Comparing this dessert with the average imitation-flavored dessert is like comparing a Rolls Royce with a thirty-year-old Model A Ford.

2 cups fresh rapsberries
or
2 packages frozen raspberries
¾ cup sugar
2 cups water
1 envelope unflavored colorless gelatin

1. Bring the raspberries, water, and sugar to a boil, reduce heat and simmer for about 20 minutes or until the fruit has dissolved into a mass.
2. Line a large strainer with cheesecloth and place the strainer over a bowl. Pour the fruit mixture through, straining so that all the seeds are removed and only the clear red liquid remains. Soften gelatin in a little cold water.
3. Return the liquid to the saucepan and add the gelatin. Stir the gelatin thoroughly so that all the grains are fully dissolved.
4. Bring the liquid to a boil for 1 minute, then remove from heat.
5. Pour into a mold of the proper size (about 1¼ pints) or into small individual cups, and chill in refrigerator.
6. When gelatin has set, unmold, and serve.

§ VARIATION: This dessert can be made with pieces of any fruit. Add banana slices, orange segments, etc. to the liquid in the mold before chilling. Garnish with grated coconut.

Iced Brandied Coffee

1 pot strong coffee
2 jiggers brandy
cream and sugar as you wish

Combine the ingredients and pour over ice cubes in a pitcher. Refrigerate until ready to serve.

LUNCH III

Fresh Artichoke, Vinaigrette
Sautéed Fillet of Sole, Hollandaise
Steamed Rice
Cucumber Salad
Raspberry Tart
Iced Meursault

Fresh Artichoke, Vinaigrette

The key element in making a success of this dish is using a French steaming platform. This little gem makes the difference between a soggy, boiled vegetable and a crisp, steamed one. The taste is retained instead of being thrown out with the water. Priced under four dollars, the steaming platform is one of the best investments you can make for your kitchen. The platform is a perforated metal circle which stands on legs about 1½ inches high. Around the edge of the circle there is a series of perforated metal leaves which serve to expand or contract the overall size of the platform, depending on the size of the pot being used.

2 fresh artichokes
1 clove garlic
1 tbps. olive oil
1 tbsp. red wine vinegar
1 tsp. cracked peppercorns
½ lemon

1. Cut off the stems of the artichokes at the base so that they sit flat. With a sharp knife, cut about ½ inch from the leaves across the top. Cut off the points of the remaining leaves (around the sides) with scissors or kitchen shears. Apply the half lemon, squeezing gently, to all the cut surfaces (to prevent discoloration).

2. In a tall, fairly narrow pot, put about 1½ inches of water, and add the garlic clove (cut up in 4 pieces),

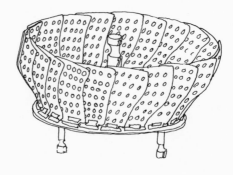

olive oil, wine vinegar, and peppercorns. Insert the steaming platform. Place the artichokes, base down, leaves up, on the platform.

3. Bring the water to a boil, cover the pot, and let the artichokes steam 25 minutes. Remove the artichokes, refrigerate them for at least two hours, and serve on a plate with a small cup of vinaigrette sauce alongside.

VINAIGRETTE SAUCE

⅓ *cup olive oil*
1 *tbsp. tarragon vinegar*
1 *tsp. Worcestershire sauce*
1 *tbsp. lemon juice*
1 *tbsp. fresh or frozen chopped chives*
½ *tsp. Lawry's Seasoned Salt*
¼ *tsp. Lawry's Seasoned Pepper*

Combine all the ingredients in a bowl and blend thoroughly. Serve as an accompaniment to the artichokes.

Sautéed Fillet of Sole, Hollandaise

2 *large fillets of sole*
1 *egg*
1 *cup milk*
½ *cup matzoh meal or dry white breadcrumbs*
2 *tbsp. olive oil*
1 *tbsp. butter*

1. In a shallow dish, beat the egg in the milk. Then let the fillets soak in the mixture for about half an hour before cooking.

2. Put two dinner plates in the oven at a low temperature to warm.

45

3. Heat a flat, pancake-type griddle or a large cast iron skillet, add oil and butter. Let the butter melt without turning brown.

4. Quickly remove the fillets from the egg and milk mixture and coat them on both sides with the matzoh meal.

5. Cook the fillets about 3 minutes on each side, no more. You will need a large spatula to turn them over without breaking. Do this carefully.

6. When the fish is done, transfer immediately to the warm plates and serve with the Hollandaise sauce.

HOLLANDAISE

There are many versions of this famous sauce, including some so-called "instant Hollandaise" recipes which, in my opinion, never come out tasting right. You need a good (preferably glass or ceramic) double boiler and a wire whisk.

> *3 large egg yolks*
> *1 tsp. lemon juice*
> *⅜ lb. butter (1½ sticks, broken into 3 equal pieces)*
> *½ tsp. salt*
> *¼ tsp. cayenne pepper*

1. Beat the egg yolks and lemon juice together in a bowl.

2. In a double boiler, place one piece of the butter over simmering water, add the egg yolk mixture, and beat *continually* with the whisk.

3. When the butter is completely melted, add a second piece and continue beating. Then add the third. When the third piece has melted and the sauce has thickened, remove from heat, stir in the salt and pepper, and transfer to sauce boat to serve with the fish.

§ NOTE: Once this sauce achieves its texture, do not reheat it or it will curdle. If it stands for some time prior to the lunch, stir it vigorously before serving.

Steamed Rice

1 cup long-grain white rice
1 tbsp. butter
1 pt. clam juice

1. Combine all the ingredients in a heavy enameled saucepan with a tightly fitting cover.
2. Bring to a boil, stir several times, then lower heat to a simmer. Cook, tightly covered, about 15 minutes or until the rice has absorbed all the liquid.
3. To keep hot until serving, leave the rice in the pan and place on an asbestos mat over very low flame or on an electric food-warming tray.
§ NOTE: The use of the clam juice precludes any need for salt, and creates a flavor which goes well with the fillet of sole.

Cucumber Salad

2 small cucumbers (or 1 large)
1 cup vinegar
½ cup lemon juice
1 tbsp. sugar
1 tsp. salt
1 tbsp. chopped chives
¼ tsp. white pepper

1. Use a potato peeler to peel the skin from the cucumbers and to slice the cucumbers into a bowl. This gives

very thin, uniform slices and is much faster than using a knife.

2. Pour the vinegar over the sliced cucumbers and let stand for at least two hours.

3. Mix the lemon juice, sugar, chives, salt, and pepper together. Drain all but approximately 1 tbsp. of the vinegar from the cucumbers, then add to the lemon dressing and serve.

Raspberry Tart

For this recipe, you will need a 6- or 7-inch round flan ring, or a 6-inch square one, and a cookie sheet. I recommend the heaviest gauge aluminum cookie sheet, because the cheap, thin ones tend to bend when exposed to heat and could crack the crust of the tart.

CRUST

> *¾ cup sifted flour*
> *1 tbsp. granulated sugar*
> *⅛ tsp. salt*
> *3 tbsp. butter*
> *1 tbsp. shortening*
> *2 tbsp. cold water*

1. Mix the dry ingredients together, then cut the butter and shortening into the flour in small pieces and toss. The resulting pieces should be about the size of corn flakes.

2. Sprinkle the dough with cold water and form it into a ball with your hands. Then on a floured board, roll it out twice to blend in the shortening and form into a ball. Wrap the dough in waxed paper and refrigerate for 2 hours (or about 1 hour in the freezer).

3. Preheat oven to 400 degrees.

4. When the dough is chilled, roll out two inches larger than your flan ring. You can check this by rolling out the dough, then gently pressing a faint outline into the surface with the flan ring. It is best to err on the side of rolling it out too large rather than too small. Roll the dough onto the rolling pin, place the flan ring on the cookie sheet, and reverse the dough onto the ring. Tuck in the corners and edges evenly. Trim any excess from the edges and save dough in case repairs are needed later. Now puncture the bottom of the dough with the tines of a fork (puncture every inch). Butter one side of a sheet of aluminum foil and tuck it into the flan ring to conform to the shape of the crust. Fill the foil with dried beans, marbles, or anything which won't burn, but will weigh down the dough.

5. Bake in the preheated oven for 10 minutes. Take from oven and remove foil with weights. Perforate the bottom of the crust again with a fork. Return to the oven for another 10 minutes, or until the crust turns a light golden color. Watch carefully during this last step; it does not harm the pastry to open the oven door and look at it. (An oven with a glass door is, of course, more convenient than one with a solid door.) When the crust is done, remove the cookie sheet from the oven and set it aside to cool, but do not remove the flan ring.

CUSTARD FILLING

½ cup sugar
3 egg yolks
6 tbsp. flour
1 cup milk
1 tbsp. butter
2 tsp. vanilla extract

1. Beat the sugar and the egg yolks together for about 5 minutes until smooth, then beat in the flour.
2. Bring the milk almost to a boil in a small saucepan. Just before the boiling point is reached, remove from heat. Start beating the egg yolk mixture again and slowly pour the hot milk into it. Now return the mixture to the saucepan and continue beating it (with a fork or wire whisk) over a low flame until it thickens. Continue beating and cooking for 2 more minutes, then remove from heat.
3. Stir in the vanilla extract and butter, then set aside and allow to cool.

FRUIT

1½ cups fresh raspberries, washed and drained
1 tbsp. powdered (confectioners') sugar

1. To assemble the tart, spread the custard filling in the pastry shell, filling it nearly to the level of the edge of the crust. Then arrange the raspberries neatly and evenly over the surface of the custard. Sprinkle with the powdered sugar and refrigerate until ready to serve.
2. To serve, lift off the flan ring and slip the tart off the cookie sheet onto a cake server or serving plate. When

removing tart from cookie sheet, it is a good idea to pass a long, flexible-bladed spatula under the tart, thus making sure it is free and not sticking to the cookie sheet.

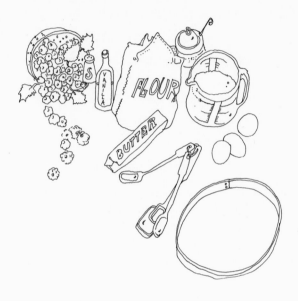

LUNCH IV

Seafood Quiche
Cold Asparagus Salad
Iced New Zealand Gooseberries
Cold Hard Cider

Seafood Quiche

You will need a 7-inch flan ring and a cookie sheet, or a 7-inch cake pan with a removable bottom and vertical sides about one inch high.

CRUST

> 1 *cup flour*
> ¼ *tsp. salt*
> 4 *tbsp. butter*
> 2 *tbsp. shortening*

1. Sift the flour and salt together into a bowl.
2. Cut the butter and the shortening into small pieces and roll them in the flour. Then add 1 or 2 tablespoons water and gather the dough into a ball. Put the ball down on a floured board and blend the shortening with the flour in the dough by pushing down with the heel of your hand, a little at a time. Scrape up the dough, mold it into a ball again, and refrigerate for several hours.

3. Butter the inside surfaces of the cake pan, or the inside of the flan ring, and the surface of the cookie sheet. Roll out cold dough so that you have a ring about ⅛ inch thick and 10 inches in diameter. Roll the dough onto your rolling pin, then reverse it onto the buttered pan. Fit the dough in carefully with your fingers, patching where necessary. Perforate the bottom at ½-inch intervals with the tines of a fork.

4. Butter one side of a piece of aluminum foil which is larger than the flan ring. Fit it into the dough, buttered side down, and fill with dried beans or other suitable weight to hold down the crust while it bakes.

5. Preheat oven to 400 degrees. Bake the crust for 10 minutes, remove it from the oven, lift out the foil and beans, perforate the bottom with a fork again, and return to the oven for another 10 minutes or until crust begins to darken slightly. Remove from oven and set aside to await filling, leaving flan ring in place.

SEAFOOD FILLING

> ¾ *cup cooked crabmeat, lobster meat, shrimps (cut in*
> *½-inch pieces), or any combination of these seafoods*
> *1 tbsp. chopped onions*
> *1 tbsp. butter*
> *¼ tsp. salt*
> *⅛ tsp. pepper*
> *2 tsp. Worcestershire sauce*
> *2 eggs*
> *½ cup heavy cream*
> *2 tsp. ketchup*
> *¼ cup grated Swiss cheese*

1. In a skillet, over medium heat, soften the onions in the butter, add the seafood, salt, pepper, and Worcestershire sauce. Simmer for 2 minutes and remove from heat.
2. Beat the eggs, cream, and ketchup together in a bowl. Then add the seafood to the bowl and mix well.
3. Pour the mixture into the crust and sprinkle the grated cheese on top.
4. Bake for 20 minutes in the 400-degree oven. When ready, top should be brown and somewhat puffed up. Remove from oven. Carefully remove flan ring or side piece of cake pan. Then slide the quiche from the cookie sheet, or the cake pan bottom, onto a serving dish. Cut into wedges like a pie and serve immediately.

§ NOTE: Try to have available a serving plate which is flat and does not have a depression in the center as many such plates do. The bottom of the quiche cannot sink down before you cut and serve it. I use a flat marble cheese platter for quiches and tarts.

Cold Asparagus Salad

1 doz. fresh green asparagus stalks
2 large lettuce leaves
¼ cup olive oil
2 tbsp. vinegar
½ tsp. salt
¼ tsp. pepper
2 strips red pimiento
2 anchovy fillets
1 finely chopped hard-cooked egg

1. Steam the asparagus on a steaming platform over boiling water in a covered pot for 20 minutes. Remove

from pot, trim thick ends down about 1 inch, and refrigerate.

2. Mix oil, vinegar, salt, and pepper to make dressing.

3. To serve, place six stalks on each plate on bed of lettuce. Pour over the mixed dressing. Then lay one strip of pimiento and one anchovy fillet diagonally across the asparagus on each plate and sprinkle with chopped egg.

Iced New Zealand Gooseberries

6 fresh New Zealand Gooseberries (or Kiwi Fruit)
½ pt. heavy cream
½ cup light brown sugar

1. Peel the fruit very carefully with a sharp paring knife, then cut each in half.

2. In a bowl, arrange the cut halves on a bed of crushed ice. Hollow out a place in the ice which will hold a small bowl of whipped cream.

3. Beat the heavy cream with an electric mixer (or hand mixer) until it forms soft peaks. Be careful not to overbeat, as the dividing line between making whipped cream and making butter is only a few seconds of beating.

4. Place a small bowl of whipped cream in the prepared place in the bed of ice.

5. Serve the fruit with brown sugar. Take a piece of fruit on a fork, dip in the whipped cream, then dip in the brown sugar before eating.

Cold Hard Cider

There are domestic, English and French brands of hard cider. Since cider doesn't travel too well, the brand names tend to be regional. In New York, there is a "Woodpecker" brand of English cider which I have used.

LUNCH V

Grilled Stuffed Mushrooms
Cold Sliced Veal
Hot Purée of Peas
Iced Cantaloupe with Sherbet
Red Wine

Grilled Stuffed Mushrooms

6 large fresh white mushrooms
2 tbsp. butter
1 tbsp. olive oil
1 cup finely chopped onion
½ cup breadcrumbs
1 tsp. parsley
¼ tsp. pepper
1 tsp. Worcestershire sauce

1. Remove the stems from the mushrooms and set aside.
2. Wash the mushroom caps by gently wiping them with a damp cloth or paper towel.
3. Wash the stems quickly in cold water and blot dry. Then chop finely.
4. Melt the butter in a small skillet and sauté the onions and chopped mushroom stems together until the onions are transparent. Stir in the breadcrumbs, parsley,

pepper, and Worcestershire sauce to make stuffing, then remove from heat.

5. In another skillet, heat the oil over medium heat, and sauté the mushroom caps for about 5 minutes (concave side up). The mushroom caps should absorb the oil and brown slightly.

6. Remove the caps from heat and allow them to cool. Stuff them with the prepared stuffing. Grill under the broiler for about 10 minutes and serve immediately. If the stuffed mushrooms start to singe around the edges during the broiling, baste with butter.

Cold Sliced Veal

1 2-lb. boneless rolled veal roast
1 medium-sized onion, sliced
1 green pepper, cut in ½-inch strips
½ tsp. white pepper

1. Preheat oven to 325 degrees.

2. Place the veal in a baking pan, surrounded by sliced onions and peppers, and rub upper surface with white pepper.

3. Roast for about 25 minutes per pound (medium) or a little longer if you prefer meat well done. Veal should *not* be rare.

4. When cooked, remove from oven, discard onions and peppers, wrap in aluminum foil, and refrigerate until ready to serve.

5. Just before serving, remove from refrigerator and slice into thin, neat slices. The meat will be much easier to slice cold than hot. Make an attractive arrangement of the slices on a serving platter and garnish with fresh parsley. Serve with mustard and/or mayonnaise.

Hot Purée of Peas

2 cups fresh green peas, shelled
2 small onions
1 small heart of lettuce
2 tbsp. butter
2 tbsp. chopped parsley
1 tsp. sugar
½ tsp. salt

1. Place all the ingredients in a saucepan with half a cup of water.
2. Cover and cook over medium heat until tender, about 15 minutes.
3. Force contents of pan through a sieve, removing any excess liquid. Keep hot and serve quickly. Butter may be added just before serving if you wish. An alternative method is to transfer the contents of the pan to a blender to purée. (If you have the type of blender which also has a heating element, here is an excuse to use it!)

Iced Cantaloupe with Sherbet

1 cantaloupe
½ pt. lime sherbet

1. Refrigerate uncut cantaloupe until a few minutes before serving.
2. Cut a little slice from the bottom of each half melon to ensure that it doesn't roll around on the plate when served.
3. Cut the cantaloupe in half, remove seeds and pulp from inside, and fill each half with a generous scoop of sherbet.

Red Wine

A light claret or Beaujolais would go well with this menu.

LUNCH VI

Cold Clabbered Milk
Hot Boiled Potatoes Garnished with
Onion and Bacon Bits
Spinach and Mushroom Salad
Strawberries Romanoff
Café Espresso

Cold Clabbered Milk

This recipe must be prepared at least a full day in advance of the meal. The ingredients are simple, but the treatment is delicate and sometimes unpredictable, depending on temperature, quality of the milk products, etc. Give it a try!

1 pt. fresh milk
½ pt. heavy cream
½ pt. sour cream
4 tbsp. unflavored yogurt

1. In a mixing bowl, beat together all the ingredients

with an electric or hand beater. Do this at the slowest speed available on the electric beater, or at a comparable speed by hand. You must mix the ingredients thoroughly, but avoid churning the mixture into buttermilk. The mixing process should not take more than a minute.

2. Pour the mixture into an attractive serving bowl or soup tureen. Cover with a damp cloth and place in a warm corner of your kitchen where it will not be disturbed for 24 hours. During this time, the cream will rise to the top and the milk will sour gently underneath, acquiring the texture of a very fragile custard.

3. About 3 hours before serving, transfer the bowl to your refrigerator and chill. Spoon into soup plates and serve the hot potatoes alongside on smaller plates. (Some people like to actually put the potatoes into the clabbered milk and eat them together.)

§ NOTE: So you will be able to check the progress of the clabbered milk, pour some into a smaller (glass) bowl when making it and set it alongside the main amount. Now you can taste or test without disturbing the surface of the one you plan to serve.

Hot Boiled Potatoes Garnished with Onion and Bacon Bits

6 strips bacon, fried crisp and crumbled
1 cup finely chopped onions
1 tbsp. olive oil
2 tbsp. butter
3 medium-sized potatoes

1. Sauté the chopped onions in the butter and olive oil until golden brown. Pour off all but about one table-

spoon of the fat, add the crumbled bacon to the onions and set aside.

2. Peel and cut in half 3 potatoes and boil them in rapidly boiling, salted water until a fork will go into one easily.

3. When the potatoes are cooked, quickly pour off the water and transfer them to a serving dish. Pour the onion and bacon mixture over them, toss lightly, and serve.

Spinach and Mushroom Salad

1 8-oz. package fresh spinach leaves
¼ lb. fresh white mushrooms
2 tbsp. olive oil
1 tbsp. vinegar
½ tsp. salt
½ tsp. pepper

1. Wash the spinach leaves with cold water and cut off any thick stalks.

2. Drain in colander.

3. Wash the mushrooms carefully with a damp paper towel or damp cloth, then cut into thin slices.

4. Mix the oil, vinegar, salt, and pepper in the salad bowl, add the mushrooms and spinach, toss thoroughly, and serve.

Strawberries Romanoff

1 pt. fresh strawberries, hulled and washed
¼ cup fresh orange juice
2 tbsp. orange liqueur
½ pt. vanilla ice cream
1 cup heavy cream, whipped

1. Put the strawberries in a bowl with the orange juice and liqueur. Let stand several hours.
2. Divide the ice cream into two dessert serving bowls. Soften ice cream until it settles evenly, then place bowls in the freezer.
3. To assemble dessert, arrange strawberries on top of the ice cream, then top with whipped cream.

Café Espresso

If you have one of the many types of steam-pressure espresso coffee pots, by all means use it with a strong, dark Italian grind of coffee.

If not, the same coffee made in a percolator or drip pot, at double strength, will achieve the same result.

LUNCH VII

Steamed Clams with Clam Broth and Drawn Butter
French Fried Potatoes
Fresh Coleslaw
Strawberry Shortcake
Iced Ale

Steamed Clams with Clam Broth and Drawn Butter

4 doz. fresh steamer clams, scrubbed
½ lb. butter

1. Steam the clams over about 1 quart of water. (See the explanation of the steamer on page 9.)

2. While the clams are steaming, melt the butter in a small saucepan, then pour the melted butter through a strainer lined with cheesecloth and keep warm until the clams are served. Do not discard the cheesecloth and strainer.

3. When the clams are partially opened and ready, remove them from the top part of the steamer and transfer them into a deep bucket or bowl lined with a large cloth napkin. Fold the napkin over the clams to keep them hot.

4. Strain the broth from the lower part of the steamer through the same cheesecloth and serve to each person in a coffee cup.

5. Also serve individual cups of the melted butter to each person. Provide an extra bowl to hold the clam shells as the clams are eaten.

French Fried Potatoes

To make french fries to perfection you need only carefully observe a few rules. First, make sure that the oil you use for frying is clean (vegetable oil is best) and at precisely the right temperature. Restaurants use expensive frying units which are equipped with thermostats to control the temperature of the fat. At home, all you need is a fat thermometer, the type with a clip on the stem which secures the thermometer to the side of the fryer, and which has an easy-to-read indicator. Second, make sure that the cut potatoes are as dry as possible. Third, before serving be sure to drain the fat which still clings to the potatoes after cooking. This is done by tossing in a paper towel. Although the shape of the french fries is optional, I recommend the classic long, thin shape, with no decorative embellishments.

> *4 medium-sized potatoes, long shapes if possible*
> *4 to 6 cups cooking oil (depending on size of fryer)*
> *salt to taste*

1. Peel the potatoes and carefully cut them into thin pieces, no more than ¼ inch square in cross section and as long as the potato allows.
2. Heat the oil in the fryer to 375 degrees, then allow the temperature to go a little higher. The reason for this is that when the cold potatoes hit the hot fat, the temperature immediately comes down. The cooking temperature should be 375 degrees, so by starting higher you reach the equilibrium sooner after putting in the potatoes.
3. While the oil is heating, spread out the potatoes to dry on paper towels.

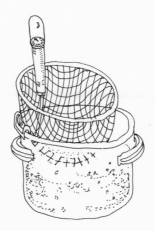

4. When the temperature is right, put the potatoes in the oil and allow them to cook until just beginning to brown. If you like them crisp, let them get a little darker; if you like them fairly soft, remove them from the oil sooner.

5. Spread the cooked potatoes out quickly on paper towels. Then pick up the edges of each towel and roll the potatoes back and forth to remove all surface oil.

6. Transfer to serving dish, sprinkle with salt, cover with a cloth and serve as soon as possible.

§ NOTE: If you start the potatoes right after putting in the lobster, they should be ready at about the same time.

Fresh Coleslaw

2 cups shredded green cabbage
½ cup finely minced onion
½ cup grated raw carrots
½ cup mayonnaise
½ tsp. salt
¼ tsp. white pepper
½ tsp. sugar
1 tbsp. lemon juice
1 tbsp. heavy cream

1. Combine all the ingredients for the dressing (mayonnaise, salt, pepper, sugar, lemon juice, cream) and mix well.

2. Toss the cabbage, onions, and carrots together in a salad bowl, pour over the dressing, toss again thoroughly and refrigerate until ready to serve.

Strawberry Shortcake

1 cup flour
1½ tsp. double-acting baking powder
¼ tsp. salt
2 tbsp. granulated sugar
4 tbsp. vegetable shortening
1 egg
6 tbsp. milk
butter for greasing cookie sheet
2 cups sliced, sugared strawberries (fresh or frozen)
½ cup heavy cream

1. Preheat oven to 450 degrees.
2. Sift the flour, baking powder, salt, and sugar together.
3. Cut the shortening into small pieces and drop into sifted ingredients. Beat egg separately and add, a little at a time, along with the milk, until the dough becomes easily malleable but not too loose. (You may not need all the milk.)
4. Shape dough into two disks, about 4 inches in diameter and ½ inch thick.
5. Place disks of dough on buttered cookie sheet, at least 2 inches apart. Bake for about 20 minutes in preheated oven or until golden.
6. When ready, remove cakes from cookie sheet and split them. Divide half of the strawberries on the two bottom halves, then replace the top halves of the cakes. Top with remaining berries.
7. Beat the heavy cream until it forms soft peaks. Crown the two strawberry shortcakes with whipped cream and serve immediately.

§ NOTE: The assembly of the cake, berries, and cream

should be done very shortly before serving so that the cake doesn't become soggy.

===

LUNCH VIII

Moules à la Poulette (Steamed Mussels in Cream Soup)
Avocado and Grapefruit Salad
Orange Cake
Coffee
Iced White Wine

===

Moules à la Poulette (Steamed Mussels in Cream Soup)

2 qts. fresh scrubbed mussels (in the shell)
2 cups chopped onions
1 bay leaf
1 tbsp. minced shallots
¾ cup white wine
2 tbsp. lemon juice
1 tsp. powdered dried mushrooms
½ pt. heavy cream
1 tbsp. chopped chives

1. Make sure all the mussels are clean and that the "beards" have been removed.
2. Cover the bottom of a heavy saucepan with the two cups of chopped onions, then add the bay leaf, and a

cup of water. Add the mussels and steam, tightly covered, for 10 minutes over medium-high heat.

3. Reduce heat to very low, uncover the pot, remove one shell from each of the mussels. Keep warm while preparing the remainder of the soup. (If any of the mussels didn't open during the steaming, discard.)

4. In a medium-sized saucepan, simmer the shallots in the white wine for about 3 minutes. Stir in the dried mushroom powder thoroughly so that it dissolves completely in the liquid.

5. Now remove the mussels from the other pot and set aside. Quickly strain the liquid from the steamed mussels into the smaller saucepan and blend.

6. Keeping the heat low, add the heavy cream and the chives to the soup. Then add the mussels and bring almost to the simmering point but *do not boil*.

7. Moules à la Poulette should be served immediately after heating, in warmed, shallow soup plates.

Avocado and Grapefruit Salad

1 *large avocado*
1 *large grapefruit (or 2 small)*
1 *tbsp. olive oil*
1 *tsp. Worcestershire sauce*
½ *tsp. salt*
¼ *tsp. pepper*

1. An avocado is perfect when it gives slightly under gentle pressure. It should not be hard and resistant, and it should not be so soft that the fingers easily sink into it. It is very important that the avocado be as close to perfection as possible.

2. Prepare the avocado by cutting it in half lengthwise,

around the large central pit. Then pry out the pit gently with a knife, avoiding rough handling which might mar the shape of the fruit. Now peel the avocado halves with a very sharp paring knife as close under the skin as possible. When each half is peeled, place it flat side down on a cutting board and carefully cut ⅛-inch slices lengthwise.

3. Cut the rind off the grapefruit with a sharp knife, making sure to remove the bitter white inner skin as well. Slice out the sections, one at a time, removing the segment skins. This process is a little wasteful, but the results are more attractive. Remove seeds while you are slicing.

4. Now arrange on your two salad plates alternating slices of avocado and grapefruit in an overlapping pattern.

5. Mix the oil, Worcestershire sauce, salt, and pepper well in a small bowl and spoon half the dressing over each salad before serving.

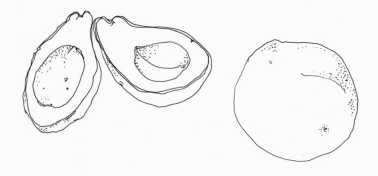

Orange Cake

This cake is larger than you need for two people. However, since it will keep beautifully for several days in the refrigerator, it makes sense to prepare the whole cake and have some extra dessert around later. For this recipe you will need two 9-inch layer cake pans, buttered and dusted with flour.

6 eggs
1 cup sugar
1 cup cake flour
½ cup melted unsalted butter
1 tsp. grated orange rind
3 tbsp. orange juice
1 tsp. vanilla extract

1. Separate the eggs. Add the vanilla extract to the yolks. Mix separately both the orange rind and orange juice with the melted butter.
2. Beat the whites until they form soft peaks, but *not stiff*. Then beat in the sugar, a little at a time, and allow the peaks to become stiff.
3. Fold the beaten whites into the yolks gently, gradually adding the melted butter and orange mixture. Be careful to do this operation gently and do not over-fold. The idea is to preserve the air bubbles trapped in the egg whites, which will give the cake its lightness. Remember, there is no baking powder or yeast in this recipe, so the whites have to bear the whole load of creating the texture.
4. Preheat oven to 350 degrees. Pour half the batter into each of the cake pans. Bake 30 minutes, until the edges of the cake pull away from the circumference of the

pans. Take immediately from the oven and carefully remove the cake layers from their pans and slip them onto a cooling rack to cool while you prepare the icing.

ICING

> *4 egg yolks*
> *4 tbsp. sugar*
> *1 tsp. vanilla extract*
> *¾ lb. softened unsalted butter*
> *2 tbsp. grated orange rind*
> *1 tbsp. orange juice*

1. Put the yolks, sugar, vanilla, orange rind, and juice into a blender.
2. Turn on blender and start adding butter, 1 tablespoon at a time. When all the butter has been added, turn off blender, transfer the icing to a bowl and refrigerate to set.
3. When the icing has chilled and the layers of the cake are cooled, you are ready to put the cake together. Spread a piece of waxed paper on your counter to catch the drippings. Slide the rack holding one of the layers onto it.
4. Spread the *top* of the bottom layer with an even layer of icing, about ¼ inch thick, or less. Do not do the sides yet. Use a long, flexible spatula.
5. Now slip the top layer onto the iced bottom layer, arranging it carefully to make sure the sides of the cake are even. (Make sure that the smoothest or best formed surface of the layers is the one which winds up being the top surface of the cake.)
6. Now put all of the icing you have left on top of the cake. Then with the spatula, using a circular motion,

spread it evenly over the top and sides. When finished, slip the cake off the rack onto a cake plate, and either serve immediately or refrigerate until about ½ hour before serving. The butter content of the icing makes it undesirable to leave the cake at room temperature for too long. Commercial cakes which you see left out much longer usually contain some sort of chemical preservative in the icing to prevent melting.

LUNCH IX

Varied Hors d'Oeuvres
Scallops in Mushroom Cream Sauce
Saffron Rice
Grilled Stuffed Tomatoes
Fresh Orange Gelatin
Coffee
Iced White Wine

Varied Hors d'Oeuvres

You may vary the ingredients according to availability and season.

73

2 *hard-cooked eggs*
½ *cup fresh crabmeat*
6 *skinless and boneless sardines*
2 *slices cooked ham*
4 *cooked jumbo shrimps*
½ *cup grated celery root*
6 *Spanish green olives stuffed with anchovies*
1 *cup mayonnaise*
1 *tsp. curry powder*
1 *tsp. tomato paste*
2 *oz. cream cheese*
1 *tsp. hot mustard*
½ *tsp. lemon juice*

1. Get out a large, attractive serving platter, and plan to arrange the hors d'oeuvres symmetrically.
2. Divide the mayonnaise into four equal ¼-cup portions in small bowls.
3. Mix the curry powder into one bowl of mayonnaise, the tomato paste into another, the mustard into the third, and the lemon juice into the fourth.
4. Place a mound of the crabmeat in the center of the platter, spoon the lemon mayonnaise over it.
5. Cut the peeled hard-cooked eggs in half, arrange them on the platter, and spoon the curry mayonnaise over them.
6. Arrange the cooked shrimps, and spoon the tomato mayonnaise over them.
7. Mix the celery root (which has been grated through the coarsest blade of your grater to create long, string-like pieces) with the mustard mayonnaise, then arrange it in a circle around the mound of crabmeat.
8. Cut the slices of ham in two, making four pieces.

Divide the cream cheese into four equal portions. Roll each piece of ham into a cone, with the cream cheese insider, and arrange on the platter.

9. Arrange the sardines and olives in the remaining spaces on the platter, refrigerate, and serve at the beginning of the lunch.

Scallops in Mushroom Cream Sauce

1 lb. (about 1 pt.) bay scallops
6 tbsp. butter
1 cup white wine
1 tbsp. chopped shallots
6 medium-to-large thinly sliced fresh mushrooms
1 tsp. flour
¼ tsp. salt
¼ tsp. white pepper

1. Place the scallops, 2 tablespoons butter, the wine, and the shallots in a saucepan. Simmer over medium

heat for about 10 minutes. Then remove the scallops and set aside. Save the liquid.

2. Add 2 more tablespoons butter and the mushrooms to the liquid. Simmer the mushrooms in the sauce for about 15 minutes over medium-low heat. The mushrooms must be soft and tender. Remove the mushrooms from the liquid with a slotted spoon and set aside, reserving the liquid.

3. In a double boiler, over simmering but not boiling water, place the remaining 2 tablespoons butter and the flour. Stir into a paste and cook for 2 or 3 minutes. Then add the cooking liquid you reserved, a little at a time, stirring continually. When all the liquid has been used, add the cooked scallops, mushrooms, salt, and pepper.

4. Leave on heat only long enough to heat through the scallops and mushrooms, then serve. The scallops and sauce may be served over the saffron rice if desired, or alongside.

Saffron Rice

1 cup long-grain white rice
2 cups cold water
2 tbsp. butter
¼ tsp. salt
½ tsp. saffron

1. Place all the ingredients in a heavy enameled saucepan which has a tightly fitting cover.

2. Bring to a boil, then reduce heat. Stir thoroughly to spread delicate yellow coloring and flavor of the saffron evenly throughout. Cover tightly and allow to simmer until all the liquid is absorbed.

3. Keep hot over low heat and tightly covered until ready to serve.

Grilled Stuffed Tomatoes

2 *large firm tomatoes*
½ *cup bread crumbs*
1 *clove garlic, put through a garlic press*
1 *tbsp. chopped onions*
1 *tbsp. chopped green pepper*
3 *tbsp. butter*
½ *tsp. salt*
½ *tsp. pepper*

1. Immerse the tomatoes for 1 minute in a saucepan of boiling water, then remove from water and set aside while preparing the stuffing.
2. Melt the butter in a saucepan, add the breadcrumbs, garlic, onions, green pepper, and seasonings. Cook over a low heat and combine all the ingredients thoroughly. Remove from heat.
3. Cut a circle about 1½ inches in diameter from the tops of the tomatoes. Scoop out insides with a spoon, leaving a shell about ¼ inch thick. Add the pulp to the stuffing mixture and stir well.
4. Now fill the tomatoes with the stuffing so that about ¼ inch of stuffing protrudes from the top.
5. About 10 minutes before serving add a pat of butter to the top of each tomato, and place under low heat in your broiler.
6. When stuffing on top has browned, remove from heat and serve immediately.

Fresh Orange Gelatin

It's easy to buy a package of artificially flavored orange gelatin, add water as the package directs, and presto, you have a dessert. Needless to say, the results are about as memorable as the effort expended. Now try my way and compare. You will need a one-quart mold, preferably ring shaped and not too high.

> *1½ cups fresh orange juice, strained*
> *2 large navel oranges, peeled and cut into sections with skins and seeds removed*
> *grated rind of the two oranges (only the colored part, not the white)*
> *½ cup granulated sugar*
> *1 tbsp. Grand-Marnier or Cointreau*
> *2 dashes orange bitters*
> *1 tsp. vanilla extract*
> *2 envelopes colorless and flavorless gelatin*

1. In an enameled saucepan, bring the orange juice to a simmer (not a boil).
2. Add the grated rind, sugar, Grand Marnier, bitters, and vanilla extract.
3. Separately, dissolve the gelatin in a little cold water until all the grains are softened.
4. Add the gelatin to the simmering juice and stir until all the gelatin is dissolved.
5. Set aside, away from heat, and allow to cool. Meanwhile, refrigerate the empty mold. When the liquid is at room temperature, pour about ⅓ of it into the mold and leave the mold in the refrigerator. (Leave the rest of the liquid out at room temperature.)
6. When the gelatin in the mold has set, remove from

refrigerator and quickly add the orange sections, evenly spaced, on the gelatin. Now fill the mold with the remaining liquid and return to the refrigerator.

7. To serve after gelatin has firmly set, dip the mold in very hot water for a few seconds, being careful to prevent any of the water from spilling into the dessert. Then reverse onto a serving plate and serve immediately.

LUNCH X

Poached Eggs in Creamed Shrimp Sauce
Steamed Rice
Asparagus Salad
Strawberry Tart
Coffee

Poached Eggs in Creamed Shrimp Sauce

4 eggs
1 lb. fresh shrimps, peeled and deveined
1 tbsp. flour
¼ lb. butter
1 pt. clam juice
1 tsp. Worcestershire sauce
½ tsp. salt
¼ tsp. white pepper
4 tbsp. heavy cream

1. Drop the shrimp into a pot of boiling water (about 2 quarts) and cook for 5 minutes until firm. Drain off water and set shrimp aside while making sauce.

2. In a double boiler over simmering water melt the butter. Then add the flour and stir with a wooden spoon until the roux (a thick paste) is formed. Allow to cook 3 minutes.

3. Now stir in the salt and pepper.

4. Begin adding the clam juice, one or two tablespoons at a time, and continue stirring the sauce. The roux will absorb the liquid. Continue until you have added most of the clam juice and the texture of the sauce is creamy and smooth but not too thick. Now stir in the Worcestershire sauce and the heavy cream. Put shrimps into the sauce and keep hot while preparing the poached eggs.

5. Poach the eggs in simmering water, remove from water with a slotted spoon, and trim. Place two eggs per portion on bed of steamed rice and spoon hot shrimp sauce over them. Serve immediately.

Steamed Rice

1 cup long-grain rice
1 tbsp. butter
1 tsp. salt
1 tsp. paprika

1. Combine the rice with 2 cups of cold water, the butter, and the salt in a heavy saucepan with a tightly fitting cover.

2. Place saucepan over high heat, and when rice is just coming to a boil, stir well to loosen any grains sticking to the bottom of the pan.

3. Reduce heat to medium-low, cover, and simmer for 14 minutes until all the liquid is absorbed.
4. Sprinkle with paprika and toss lightly just before serving.

Asparagus Salad

12 stalks fresh green asparagus
2 large lettuce leaves
2 tbsp. olive oil
1 tbsp. vinegar
½ tsp. salt
¼ tsp. pepper
½ tsp. finely minced garlic
½ tsp. finely minced chives
½ finely chopped hard-cooked egg

1. Steam the asparagus over boiling water for 12 minutes in a steamer. (Make sure you first trim off the hard thick ends of the stalks.)
2. Drain and refrigerate the asparagus.
3. Arrange one leaf of the lettuce, washed and patted dry with a paper towel, on each of two individual salad plates.
4. Mix the rest of the ingredients together in a bowl, adding the chopped egg last. Stir it in gently.
5. When the asparagus is chilled, arrange 6 stalks on each lettuce leaf, spoon over the sauce, and serve.

Strawberry Tart

Follow the directions for the Raspberry Tart in Lunch III, page 48, substituting 1½ cups hulled and washed fresh strawberries for the raspberries.

Thirty Dinners
for Two

~~~

DINNER I
Bouillabaisse
Hot Garlic Bread
Compote of Pears
White Wine

~~~

Bouillabaisse

Bouillabaisse is the traditional French fish soup or stew. It is a whole meal in itself and is rarely followed by another course, other than a light dessert. The French use fish which are available only in the Mediterranean, so any American version will lack authenticity. However, the substitution of different fish does not detract from the excellence of bouillabaisse as a meal.

4-lb. mixture of cod slices, striped bass, mackerel, salmon, porgy, flounder, or any other fresh ocean fish, cleaned, with heads and tails removed

1 small live Maine lobster (if possible) or 1 package of frozen lobster tails

1 doz. fresh shrimps

½ cup chopped onion

1 chopped tomato

4 tbsp. tomato paste

2 cloves garlic, peeled and chopped

1 tsp. saffron

1 tbsp. freshly chopped parsley

1 bay leaf

¼ cup olive oil

½ tsp. pepper

½ tsp. salt

1. Parboil the lobster for about 5 minutes, remove from water, allow to cool slightly for ease of handling, then split the tail, and cut it into sections. Split open the claws. The lobster goes into the bouillabaisse along with the other fish.

2. Put all the fish, the lobster, and the shrimps (which should be peeled and cleaned, but not yet cooked), in a large, heavy enameled stew pot.

3. Add all the remaining ingredients and then pour in enough cold water to cover by about ½ inch.

4. Bring to a boil and then reduce heat. Let the soup simmer for 15 minutes, then remove from heat and serve.

5. If you have the large-sized European-type soup plates, which tend to be larger and deeper than American ones, put a slice of the hot garlic bread in each plate and pour the soup over it. On another dish, preferably warmed, serve the pieces of fish, lobster, and shrimps.

Hot Garlic Bread

> 1 8- to 10-inch loaf Italian bread
> 1 clove garlic, peeled
> 4 tbsp. butter
> 2 tbsp. grated Parmesan cheese

1. Mince the garlic.

2. Melt the butter over low heat, add the minced garlic, and cook for 4 minutes.

3. Divide the loaf of bread lengthwise in half.

4. Spread the melted garlic butter evenly over the cut faces of the bread.

5. Sprinkle 1 tablespoon of the Parmesan over each half loaf, then place the bread under the oven broiler for about

2 minutes or until the bread toasts to a golden brown and the cheese sizzles but does not burn.

6. Serve in a basket covered with a cloth to keep warm. Note: If you are using a piece of the bread in the soup as suggested, cut a 2-inch piece off each half loaf, and serve the rest of the bread in the basket as described.

Compote of Pears

2 large (or 4 small) cooking pears
1 tbsp. lemon juice
½ cup sugar
1 tsp. vanilla extract
1 cup water

1. Peel the pears very carefully, cut in quarters or halves, depending on size, and remove the cores and stems.
2. Place the peeled pears in a bowl and baste several times with the lemon juice. Let stand 15 minutes and repeat the process.
3. In a saucepan bring the water, sugar, and vanilla to a boil. Then reduce heat, add the pears, and simmer for about 10 minutes. They should cook but remain fairly firm. If they soften too quickly (this depends on ripeness and size), stop the cooking sooner.
4. The compote may be served hot or chilled.

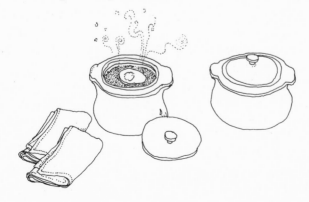

~❧~

DINNER II
Grilled Ham Steak
Raisin Gravy
Buttered Sweet Potatoes
Zucchini
Hot Corn Biscuits
Pumpkin Pie
Cold Ale

~❧~

Grilled Ham Steak

2 one-half inch thick ham steaks
fresh pepper
2 tsp. olive oil

1. For this recipe the best implement is a cast iron or aluminum stove-top grill. It resembles a fairly flat frying pan with raised ridges in the bottom and a runoff channel for the drippings to one side. Heat the grill until it is very hot (a drop of water should bounce on it), brush the ham steaks with olive oil on both sides and then sprinkle both sides with pepper.

2. Place the steaks on the grill and cook each side for 10 to 12 minutes, turning several times in the process. If the ridges of the grill are making too deep a burn in the steaks, reduce the heat considerably for 3 or 4 minutes, then return to high.

3. The steaks should be grilled after the gravy is made. The ham drippings can be added to the gravy at the last minute.

Raisin Gravy

1 cup raisins (half large white Sultana and half dark raisins)
2 cups apple juice
1 tbsp. soy sauce (use the Japanese rather than the Chinese; it is less salty)
1 tsp. hot mustard
2 tbsp. sugar
drippings from the grilled ham steaks

1. Bring the apple juice, soy sauce, mustard, and sugar to a boil in an enameled saucepan. Boil for 4 or 5 minutes until there is a noticeable thickening.
2. Add the raisins and simmer another 10 minutes. Then reduce heat to very low and keep hot.
3. After removing the ham steaks from the grill, pour the drippings into the gravy, stir, and raise heat to a simmer for about a minute before transferring to a gravy boat for the table.

Buttered Sweet Potatoes

2 sweet potatoes or yams
2 tbsp. butter
1 tbsp. brown sugar
1 tsp. lemon juice

1. Bake the potatoes in a 450-degree oven for 1 hour.
2. Remove from oven, split in half lengthwise, and lay flat on shallow broiling pan, cut sides up.
3. Soften the butter, mix with the brown sugar into a paste, then spread the paste evenly over the cut sides of the potatoes. Sprinkle with the lemon juice and put the

potatoes under the broiler, set on low heat for 8 to 10 minutes.

4. When butter and sugar mixture has melted and formed a glaze, remove from broiler and serve immediately.

Zucchini

This vegetable resembles a medium-sized cucumber in appearance and is its relative. Zucchini is a form of squash, and it is a delicious and tender hot vegetable.

> 2 zucchini
> 2 tbsp. butter
> 4 tbsp. grated Parmesan cheese
> 1 tsp. Maggi seasoning
> ½ tsp. Lawry's Seasoned Salt

1. Drop the zucchini, unpeeled, into boiling water and boil for 10 minutes.

2. Preheat oven to 350 degrees.

3. Using tongs remove the zucchini from the boiling water and cut them in half lengthwise.

4. Spread the exposed surfaces with the butter and sprinkle evenly with the seasoned salt, then the cheese, then the Maggi.

5. Place in baking dish and bake for about 10 minutes. Just before serving, slip the pan under the broiler for a minute or so to lightly brown the cheese. Serve immediately.

Hot Corn Biscuits

½ cup milk
½ cup cornmeal
2 tbsp. softened butter
½ tsp. salt
½ cup flour
3 tsp. baking powder

1. In a bowl, mix the cornmeal, butter, and salt together.
2. In a saucepan, bring the milk almost to a boil, then just before the boiling point is reached, pour into the cornmeal mixture. Allow this mixture to cool.
3. Preheat oven to 425 degrees.
4. Sift the flour and baking powder together into the cooled cornmeal mixture. Stir well until the flour is blended in.
5. Roll out the dough on a floured board to a thickness of about 1 inch. Cut into round biscuits with a 1½-inch-diameter cutter. Place well apart on a dry cookie sheet and bake for 20 minutes in the preheated oven. Remove and serve in bread basket covered by a napkin to keep hot.

Pumpkin Pie

CRUST

1 cup flour
½ tsp. salt
4 tbsp. vegetable shortening
3 tbsp. cold water

1. Sift the flour and salt together into a bowl. Now cut the shortening into the flour. The mixture should have the appearance of corn flakes.

2. Sprinkle the water over the dough, mix well, knead with your hands, and form into a ball. Wrap in waxed paper and refrigerate to chill.

3. When the dough is chilled, roll it out on a floured board, then line a 9-inch pie dish (Pyrex) or pan, making holes in the bottom with a fork. Refrigerate the lined pan until ready to fill.

4. Preheat oven to 325 degrees.

FILLING

> 2 cups cooked pumpkin flesh, fresh or canned
> ¾ cup brown sugar
> 1 tsp. cinnamon powder
> ½ tsp. salt
> ⅔ cup milk
> 2 beaten eggs
> 1 cup heavy cream

1. In a large mixing bowl, mix the pumpkin, brown sugar, cinnamon, and salt.

2. Using an electric mixer or hand beater, beat in the remaining ingredients.

3. Pour the mixture into the lined pie pan and bake in the preheated oven for 1 hour and 10 minutes. To test, insert cake needle or thin knife into filling. It should come out clean and dry.

DINNER III
Paëlla Marinera
Lettuce Salad with Lemon Chive Dressing
Flan
Iced Sangria

Paëlla Marinera

½ lb. cooked lobster meat
¼ lb. cooked shrimps
1 doz. raw littleneck clams
½ pt. mussels
2 chicken legs
1 clove garlic, crushed
½ tsp. salt
2 tbsp. olive oil
1 tsp. vinegar
4 slices bacon, cut into 1-inch pieces
½ cup chopped onion
½ cup chopped green pepper
1 tbsp. tomato paste
1 cup rice
¼ tsp. saffron

1. Mix together the crushed garlic, 1 teaspoon the olive oil, salt, and vinegar. Coat the chicken legs with the mixture, then brown them in a deep skillet in the remaining olive oil. Now add the bacon, chopped onion, and green pepper and cook slowly until onion begins to brown

93

slightly (about 5 minutes). Now add the tomato paste and the uncooked rice and cook another 5 minutes.

2. Add 2 cups of water and the saffron, turn up heat and cook until the rice absorbs the liquid. Watch carefully. You should stir only once, when the liquid is almost completely absorbed.

3. In a separate pan, steam the mussels and clams over boiling water until the shells open. Rinse them to make sure all the sand is removed. Discard any mussel or clam whose shell did *not* open. Add them to the skillet. Add lobster meat and shrimps. Cover the skillet and cook for another 10 minutes.

4. The best way to serve paëlla is to bring the skillet to the table, place it on a trivet, and serve directly onto dinner plates from there.

Lettuce Salad with Lemon Chive Dressing

The main thing to be sure of in preparing this simple salad is that you use only the most tender, pale green bibb lettuce and the freshest possible chives.

1 head fresh bibb lettuce
2 tbsp. fresh chopped chives (¼-inch pieces)
3 tbsp. olive oil
1 tbsp. lemon juice
¼ tsp. salt
¼ tsp. white pepper
½ tsp. sugar

1. Wash and separate the lettuce leaves, drain thoroughly, and tear into 1-inch pieces.

2. In a salad bowl, mix the oil, lemon juice, salt, pepper, and sugar well. Stir in the chopped chives.

3. To serve, add the lettuce and toss well.

94

Flan

¼ cup sugar
⅛ tsp. salt
½ tsp. vanilla extract
2 eggs
2 tbsp. cold milk
1 cup hot milk

1. Cook all but 1 tablespoon of the sugar in a small saucepan until it turns a golden caramel color.
2. Divide the caramel equally between two Pyrex custard cups and coat the bottom and sides of the cups. This has to be done quickly before the sugar hardens. Set the cups aside.
3. Mix the vanilla, salt, and remaining sugar. Beat in the eggs and cold milk.
4. Now slowly pour in the hot milk, beating all the while.
5. Preheat oven to 325 degrees.
6. Pour the mixture into the custard cups. Set the cups in a shallow pan of water about ¾ inch deep and bake for about 1 hour. The custard is ready when a cake needle inserted in the center comes out clean.
7. After cooking, allow the custard to cool, then refrigerate.
8. To serve, turn the custard out upside down onto individual plates.

Iced Sangria

This is the classic Spanish wine punch, and there are many variations. Try my variation the first time, then you can change it to suit your own taste.

1 orange
1 lemon
½ cup orange juice
¼ cup lemon juice
½ cup sugar
½ tsp. orange bitters
1 bottle (4/5 qt.) red Rioja or similar red wine

1. Slice the orange and the lemon into round, paper-thin slices.

2. Put the slices and all the other ingredients in a pitcher large enough to allow room for the addition of ice cubes.

3. Mix thoroughly, making sure the sugar is completely dissolved. If you have some superfine granulated bar sugar, use it instead of the regular granulated kind.

4. Refrigerate the sangria. Fill the pitcher with ice cubes when ready to serve dinner.

5. It is traditional to serve the sangria with a large wooden spoon in the pitcher for stirring before pouring.

§ NOTE: To increase the potency of this punch without disturbing the flavor, add a couple of jiggers (or more) of vodka. You'll never know it was there—nor will your guest—until later!

DINNER IV

Boiled Knackwurst
Sauerkraut
Steamed Buttered Potatoes
Cucumber Salad
Apple Pancake
Dark Beer

Boiled Knackwurst

The key element here is finding a good German deli-catessen or butcher who carries real knackwurst. Knack-wurst is a delicious pork sausage that's about twice as big around and a little shorter than a frankfurter.

4 knackwurst
hot mustard

1. Bring a medium-sized saucepan of lightly salted water to a strong rolling boil.
2. Separate the knackwurst (if they are in a chain) and punch a few small holes through the skins to prevent splitting.
3. Drop them into the boiling water and boil for 10 minutes.
4. Remove from water and serve piping hot with mustard.

Sauerkraut

The best kind of sauerkraut to buy is freshly made and stands in big wooden barrels in a good German delicatessen. However, acceptable substitutes are packaged in plastic bags or canned and are available in the super-market.

> 1 qt. sauerkraut
> 3 tbsp. butter
> 3 strips bacon, cut in 1-inch pieces
> 1 small, tart apple, not peeled, but cored and cut into 6 or 8 wedges
> 1 tbsp. tomato paste
> 1 tbsp. brown sugar
> 10 whole peppercorns
> 1 bay leaf

1. Combine all of the ingredients in a fairly deep sauce-pan. Bring to a simmer over medium heat.
2. Cover and simmer at low heat at least 30 minutes. More time is permissible.
3. The sauerkraut may be kept hot and served anytime. The longer it cooks, the better it tastes.

Steamed Buttered Potatoes

> 2 large potatoes, peeled and cut in half
> 1 tbsp. butter
> 1 tsp. chopped parsley
> 1 tsp. salt

1. Steam the potatoes over boiling water on a steaming platform for at least 20 minutes, until they are cooked through. (Be careful to watch the water level. It may be necessary to add some water halfway through to avoid burning the pan.)
2. Remove the potatoes from the pan and put them in a serving dish.

3. Add the butter, salt, and parsley and toss the potatoes until the butter is almost melted and the parsley adheres to the potatoes. Serve hot.

Cucumber Salad

2 large cucumbers
1 cup sour cream
1 tbsp. hot mustard
½ tsp. Lawry's Seasoned Salt
3 dashes Worcestershire sauce

1. Peel the cucumbers, then slice them very thin with a knife or the large slicing blade on a standard grater.
2. Mix the remaining ingredients thoroughly in a salad bowl.
3. Stir in the sliced cucumbers and refrigerate until ready to serve.
4. Just before serving you may toss them again and garnish with a little chopped parsley or chives for a decorative effect.

Apple Pancake

This wonderful dessert should be cooked and served immediately, so don't do it until after you have finished the main course of the dinner. You can complete the first three steps in advance so that all there is left to do is the final preparation, which takes no more than 5 or 6 minutes.

1 egg
½ cup sifted flour
⅛ tsp. salt
1 tsp. sugar
½ cup milk
4 tbsp. unsalted butter
4 tbsp. powdered cinnamon and 4 tbsp. granulated
  sugar mixed together in a shaker
juice of ½ lemon
2 ripe apples

1. Beat the egg, flour, salt, sugar, and milk together until you have a smooth batter.
2. Peel and core the apples, then cut them into ½-inch cubes.
3. Arrange the bowl of batter, the apples, the cinnamon-sugar shaker, the butter, and the lemon half conveniently near the stove to have everything handy for preparation.
4. In a large iron frying pan, melt the butter and spread it all over the surface and sides of the pan. Do not allow it to burn. Pour in about 3 or 4 tablespoons of batter, and quickly tilt the pan around so that the batter spreads evenly. This must be done quickly before the batter sets. Cook for about 1 minute.
5. Now spread the apples all over the surface of the batter and spoon on 3 more tablespoons of batter.
6. Using your biggest spatula, carefully turn the whole pancake over to cook the other side. This should take another minute or two at the most.
7. Turn off heat. Roll the pancake up in the pan like an omelette and transfer to serving platter. Sprinkle it with the lemon juice, then with the cinnamon-sugar. At the table, cut in half and serve.

〜ᛞ〜

DINNER V
New England Style Clam Chowder
Steamed Alaskan King Crab with
Drawn Butter
Fresh Corn on the Cob
Coleslaw
Fresh Peach Cake
Ice-Cold Beer

〜ᛞ〜

New England Style Clam Chowder

12 fresh medium-sized littleneck or cherrystone clams
2 tbsp. olive oil
½ cup finely chopped onion
1 large potato, peeled and cut into small cubes
½ tsp. salt
¼ tsp. white pepper
½ cup milk
½ cup heavy cream

1. Scrub the clams with a brush under cold running water.
2. Place them in a saucepan, cover with cold water, and boil until the shells open. Remove the clams from the liquid and retain the liquid after straining it through cheesecloth.
3. Remove the clams from the shells, wash them under running water, and chop them.
4. Heat the olive oil in a saucepan. Saute the onions

until they brown slightly, then add the clams, clam broth, potatoes, salt, and pepper.

5. Simmer until the potatoes are cooked through but still firm. Finally add the milk and the cream, bring back to just barely simmering. Serve immediately.

§ OPTIONAL: Add a couple dashes of Worcestershire sauce or Maggi seasoning.

Steamed Alaskan King Crab with Drawn Butter

In most of the world, if you want Alaskan king crab you have to buy it frozen. So unless you live in Alaska, Seattle, or Western Canada, that's what you must do for this recipe. But don't worry, the crab does not lose flavor or freshness in the quick freezing process.

> 1 *lb. Alaskan king crabmeat, without shell (if in shell,*
>   *double the weight)*
> 1 *clove garlic, cut into 4 pieces*
> 1 *tbsp. olive oil*
> 5 *cracked peppercorns*
> 1 *bay leaf*
> ⅛ *lb. butter (½ stick)*

1. Place the crabmeat on a steaming platform in a deep saucepan or pot over water containing the garlic, olive oil, peppercorns, and bay leaf.
2. Cover and steam for 20 minutes.
3. While the steaming is going on, melt the butter. When the butter is melted, strain it through cheesecloth to remove white sediment and transfer into two custard cups.

4. Serve the crab with the melted butter on the side for dipping.

Fresh Corn on the Cob

4 ears fresh corn
1 tbsp. sugar
4 tbsp. butter
shaker of seasoned salt

1. Strip the corn and break off the stems evenly.
2. In a large pot, bring plenty of water to a boil, and add the sugar to it.
3. Drop the corn in and boil no more than 5 minutes.
4. Transfer to serving dish and cover with a napkin to keep hot.
5. Serve immediately with butter and seasoned salt.

Coleslaw

½ head cabbage, firm and fresh
½ cup finely chopped onion
1 tbsp. lemon juice
1 tsp. sugar
½ cup mayonnaise
¼ cup sour cream
½ tsp. salt
½ tsp. fresh white pepper

1. Grate the cabbage (or cut) into ⅛- to ¼-inch sections. Toss cabbage with chopped onion, salt, and pepper.
2. Combine mayonnaise, sour cream, sugar, and lemon juice in a bowl and blend thoroughly. Then pour over cabbage mixture in larger bowl and mix well. Refrigerate until ready to serve.

Fresh Peach Cake

DOUGH

> 1 *cup flour*
> 2 *tsp. double-acting baking powder*
> ¼ *tsp. salt*
> 1 *tbsp. sugar*
> 4 *tbsp. butter*
> 1 *egg*
> ¼ *cup milk*

1. Sift the dry ingredients together into a mixing bowl.
2. With two knives cut the butter into the flour mixture to form small flakes. Stir.
3. Beat the egg and milk together. Add, a little at a time, to the dough, kneading it lightly.
4. On a lightly floured board, knead the dough a few more times, roll out to a thickness of about ½ inch. Line a 6-inch-square Pyrex baking dish with the dough. You may use a round dish with the same capacity.

FILLING

> 3 *fresh ripe peaches, peeled and sliced into ¼-inch-thick slices*
> ¼ *cup sugar*
> 1 *tbsp. flour*
> ½ *cup sour cream*
> ½ *cup peach or apricot preserves*

1. Preheat oven to 350 degrees.
2. Arrange peach slices on the dough in the pan.
3. Mix the remaining ingredients together thoroughly, spoon over the peaches.

4. Bake for 45 minutes in the preheated oven, then take out and allow to cool. Serve directly from baking pan.

DINNER VI

Caviar Le Roux
Consommé with Liver Dumplings
Creamed Shrimps
Mashed Peas
Tiny Onions with Parsley
Cherries Jubilée
Coffee

Caviar Le Roux

I learned of this unique recipe during a conversation at a very elegant lunch in Switzerland. Trust the Swiss to come up with a superbly crafted design using the most precious material!

8 oz. beluga or sevruga caviar
2 eggs, at room temperature
½ cup good cognac or brandy

1. Use enough water to cover the two eggs and bring to a boil in a small saucepan.
2. Using a clock or watch with a second hand, boil the eggs for exactly 30 seconds and remove immediately from the water. (I recommend using slotted spoon, wire basket, or tongs to allow you to lower the eggs into the boiling water at the precise moment and remove them at the precise moment without any hesitation.)

3. With a sharp knife, or even better, with an egg cutter, cut off ¼ inch from the rounded ends of the eggs (not the pointed ends).

4. Pour out all the egg white without allowing the yolk to fall out. If it does, start all over again—what's a wasted egg or two compared to the cost of the caviar?

5. Now carefully, with a spoon small enough to fit through the opening in the egg without risking damage to the remaining shell, fill the eggs with caviar.

6. To serve, you will need two small metal stands, the type made to support irregularly shaped art objects such as geodes. Divide the cognac into two saucers, then place one egg on each stand in the cognac and bring the saucers to the table. At table, flame the cognac and let it burn until the caviar pushes up about ¼ inch above the top edge of the shells. Then blow out the flame. The caviar and egg yolk are eaten directly from the shell, using a small spoon.

Consommé with Liver Dumplings

To make real consommé from "scratch" requires patience and time. It is well worth the effort, but sometimes when time is lacking, a canned consommé may be used with success.

CONSOMMÉ

> 1 *lb. lean beef*
> *beef bones*
> 1 *chicken carcass*
> 1 *cup sliced carrots*
> ½ *cup sliced turnip*
> ½ *cup sliced leeks*
> 1 *stalk celery, sliced*
> 1 *medium-sized onion, peeled*
> 2 *qts. water*

Assemble all of the ingredients in a deep stock pot and simmer very gently for 4 hours. If the stock reduces too quickly, add a little water. When the stock is tasty and lightly colored, remove from stove and refrigerate until all the fat has risen to the surface. Then remove the fat with a spoon, reheat the stock, and strain to remove bones and vegetables. You now have a fine consommé, which needs only a little additional salt.

LIVER DUMPLINGS

> 1 *tbsp. butter*
> 2 *eggs*
> 2 *tbsp. finely ground raw calves liver*
> 2 *tbsp. matzoh meal or very fine bread crumbs*

1. Separate the eggs.
2. Cream the egg yolks with the butter to make a smooth mixture. Add the liver and mix again. Now stir in the matzoh meal.
3. Beat the egg whites in a separate bowl until soft peaks are formed.

4. Now bring the consommé to a slow simmer. Mix the beaten egg whites into the liver mixture thoroughly.

5. Drop the dumpling batter, 1 teaspoon at a time, into the simmering soup. When all the dumplings are done, cover the consommé and let it cook for 3 minutes. Serve hot.

Creamed Shrimps

Follow the recipe for Coquilles St. Jacques in Dinner XIX, page 167, substituting 1 pound fresh raw shrimps, peeled and washed, for the scallops and using ¾ cup crème fraîche instead of only 2 tablespoons.

Mashed Peas

1½ cups fresh large peas, shelled
3 small onions
1 sprig parsley
½ tsp. dried chervil
2 tsp. salt
1 tbsp. sugar
3 tbsp. butter
½ cup heavy cream

1. In a deep saucepan. stir all the ingredients together and add ½ cup of water.

2. Bring the mixture to a boil, then reduce heat, cover, and simmer for 15 minutes.

3. Either rub the cooked mixture through a strainer and then mix the cream in vigorously, or put the mixture in a blender with the cream and blend about 20 seconds or until the purée is uniform in color.

4. Return to the saucepan to keep warm (over very

low heat) until serving time, or serve immediately after blending.

§ NOTE: If you happen to own one of those blenders which also has a heating element, it is ideal for finishing this dish, because it eliminates the transfer back to the saucepan.

Tiny Onions with Parsley

18 very small onions
1 tbsp. chopped fresh parsley
½ cup white wine
1 tbsp. butter
½ tsp. salt

1. Peel the onions carefully, just removing the outer, dry skin.
2. Simmer the onions in a small saucepan with the wine, butter, and salt for about 15 minutes, or until they are tender but not disintegrating. (The cooking time depends upon the size of the onions, so you will have to keep an eye on them.)
3. When cooked, sprinkle the chopped parsley over them and serve.

§ NOTE: The onions may be kept warm after preparation without any damage to the taste.

Cherries Jubilée

This dessert always looks beautiful and is relatively simple to prepare.

1 pt. vanilla ice cream
1 cup canned or frozen pitted dark cherries
1 tsp. sugar
½ tsp. arrowroot
2 tbsp. kirsch

1. Divide the ice cream into two portions on dessert plates, and keep them in the freezer until serving time.
2. In a small saucepan, mix the juice from the cherries with the arrowroot, and stir until the arrowroot is completely dissolved. Add the sugar, then cook over low heat until just short of the boiling point (2 or 3 minutes).
3. Add the cherries, and warm another 2 or 3 minutes. Separately, warm the kirsch by holding it over a flame in a large ladle or small saucepan for about a minute.
4. Transfer the cherries with their liquid to a serving bowl.
5. Serve the ice cream. At the last moment, pour the kirsch into the cherries and ignite it, then pour the flaming cherries in their sauce over the ice cream.

<hr />

DINNER VII

Prosciutto and Melon
Chicken Oregano and White Wine Sauce
Risotto Milanese
Green Salad
Zabaglione
Red Wine

<hr />

Prosciutto and Melon

This is an excellent and refreshing first course, and its success depends entirely on the quality of the ingredients and not on cooking skill of any kind. First you must find an Italian delicatessen or butcher shop where real Italian prosciutto is available, not the American imitations or the frequently used substitute, German West-phalian ham. Also important is the ripeness and firmness of the melon. Cantaloupe is perfect, but any other sweet melon, except watermelon, will do nicely.

> 1 *cantaloupe, seeded, peeled and cut into ½-inch × 2-inch pieces*
> ½ *lb. prosciutto, cut into paper-thin slices*
> 2 *lemon wedges*
> *pepper mill containing black pepper*

1. Trim the fat from the slices of prosciutto.
2. Cut the prosciutto into pieces large enough to wrap around the pieces of melon one and a half times.
3. Wrap the melon with the prosciutto and secure each piece with a toothpick.
4. Serve with a lemon wedge and a turn of freshly ground pepper.

Chicken Oregano and White Wine Sauce

> 1 *3-lb. fryer, cut into sections*
> 3 *tbsp. olive oil*
> 1 *tbsp. oregano*
> ½ *cup concentrated chicken broth*
> ½ *cup white wine*
> 2 *tbsp. butter*
> 1 *tbsp. flour*
> ½ *tsp. salt*
> ¼ *tsp. white pepper*

1. Heat the olive oil in a large skillet. Then brown the pieces of chicken over high heat. When browned on all sides, reduce heat to low, add oregano and 2 tablespoons

of the wine to the skillet, cover, and simmer for 45 minutes.

2. When the chicken is almost cooked, melt the butter in the top of a double boiler over simmering water. Add the flour to the melted butter and stir with a wooden spoon until a paste is formed. Slowly stir in the wine, then the chicken broth, a little at a time, to form the sauce.

3. Pour the sauce over the chicken in the skillet and stir it into the chicken juices.

4. Transfer chicken and sauce into serving dish and serve hot.

Risotto Milanese

3 tbsp. butter
1 tbsp. finely chopped onion
½ cup rice
½ tsp. saffron
1 cup chicken broth
¼ tsp. salt
¼ tsp. pepper
½ cup grated Parmesan cheese

1. In a large skillet, simmer the chopped onion in 2 tablespoons of butter. Add the rice and cook until the rice is dry.

2. Add the broth and the saffron to the rice and bring to a boil. Season with salt and pepper, reduce heat, cover, and cook for 20 minutes.

3. Just before serving, add the remaining butter in small pieces to surface of rice and sprinkle with the grated Parmesan. Serve hot.

Green Salad

1 small head bibb lettuce
1 small bunch watercress
1 tbsp. chopped parsley
1 tsp. chopped chives
2 tbsp. olive oil
1 tbsp. vinegar
1 tsp. lemon juice
½ tsp. salt
½ tsp. pepper

1. Wash and tear the lettuce and set it to drain in a colander. Wash and separate the watercress, trim off any thick stalks, and add it to the lettuce.
2. Mix the chopped chives and parsley together and set aside.
3. In a wooden bowl, mix the oil, vinegar, lemon juice, salt, and pepper.
4. Just before serving, add the salad to the bowl, toss, and finish off by sprinkling with the parsley-chive mixture.

Zabaglione

5 egg yolks
5 tbsp. sugar
½ envelope inflavored gelatin
1 tbsp. water
½ cup Marsala wine
2 maraschino cherries
1 small bar unsweetened chocolate

1. Soften the gelatin in the water in a Pyrex cup, then melt by placing the cup into hot (simmering) water.

2. Away from heat, beat the egg yolks with a wire whisk in the top of a double boiler, then gradually add the sugar and wine and continue beating.

3. Now place the top over the bottom section of the double boiler and continue beating the mixture over hot water until it thickens and gets foamy. Remove from heat, then beat in the softened gelatin.

4. Pour the mixture into coffee cups or two-handled soup cups. Refrigerate for several hours.

5. Before serving, add a maraschino cherry and shave some unsweetened chocolate over the top of each cup of zabaglione.

DINNER VIII

Iced Clam and Tomato Juice
Broiled Whole Maine Lobster with
Crabmeat Stuffing
French Fried Potatoes
Mixed Salad
Ice-Cold Beer

Iced Clam and Tomato Juice

½ pt. tomato juice
½ pt. clam juice
1 tbsp. Worcestershire sauce
1 dash Tabasco sauce
1 tbsp. lemon juice
¼ tsp. salt

1. Combine all ingredients in a cocktail shaker or blender.
2. Shake or blend for 30 seconds.
3. Serve in tall glasses over cracked ice. Garnish with lemon wedge, if desired.

Broiled Whole Maine Lobster with Crabmeat Stuffing

2 *live 1- to 1½-lb. Maine lobsters, split in half (have the fish market do the splitting)*
½ lb. cooked fresh crabmeat
½ cup breadcrumbs
2 *tbsp. butter (for stuffing)*
½ cup melted butter (to brush lobster before cooking)
½ cup melted butter (to serve with lobster)
½ tsp. salt

1. Melt the 2 tablespoons butter in a small skillet, stir in the breadcrumbs followed by the crabmeat. Mix well quickly and remove from heat.
2. Divide the stuffing into two portions, and stuff the cavities in the split lobsters. Dot the top of the stuffing with additional butter and brush all the top surfaces with the melted butter. Sprinkle on salt.
3. Turn broiler to high, and let the oven heat for about 5 minutes before putting in lobsters.
4. Broil the lobsters about 4 inches away from the heat for about 20 minutes, or until the ends of the claws just barely begin to char.
5. Remove from heat and serve with melted butter in small cups with each portion.

French Fried Potatoes

Follow the recipe for french fries in Lunch VII, page 64.

Mixed Salad

1 *head fresh lettuce*
1 *large, firm tomato, sliced*
1 *cucumber, peeled and thinly sliced*
1 *avocado, pitted, peeled, and sliced*
4 *¼-inch slices Bermuda onion*
8 *pitted green olives*
3 *tbsp. olive oil*
1 *tbsp. vinegar*
½ *tsp. salt*
¼ *tsp. pepper*

1. In a salad bowl, mix together the oil, vinegar, salt, and pepper.
2. Wash and drain the lettuce, and tear into 1½-inch pieces.
3. Add all the salad ingredients to the dressing, toss, and serve.

§ NOTE: It might be best to serve the salad before the lobster to allow full attention to the lobster when it arrives at the table.

Hot Apple Fritters

BATTER

1 *cup flour*
1 *tsp. double-acting baking powder*
½ *tsp. salt*
2 *tbsp. sugar*
1 *beaten egg*
⅔ *cup milk*
1 *tbsp. melted butter*

1. Sift the flour, salt, sugar, and baking powder together.
2. Mix the egg, milk, and melted butter together, then stir into the sifted ingredients. Beat with hand-held egg-beater to blend thoroughly and get all lumps of flour dissolved.
3. Set aside to await preparation of fritters.

APPLES

> *2 firm, tart apples, not overripe*
> *2 tbsp. sugar*
> *¼ tsp. cinnamon*
> *2 tbsp. apple juice*

1. Peel and core the apples, then cut them into round slices (with a hole in the middle).
2. Put the slices in a bowl, mix the sugar and cinnamon together, then sprinkle over the apple slices. Sprinkle on the apple juice and allow the apples to marinate in the liquid for 2 hours.

FINAL PREPARATION:

> *4 to 6 cups cooking oil*

1. Heat cooking oil in deep fryer to 375 degrees.
2. To cook the fritters, dip apple slices one at a time in the batter, and then deep fry for 3 or 4 minutes, or until golden brown. Drain on a paper towel and serve hot, sprinkled with a little additional sugar.

DINNER IX

Cold Russian Borscht
Blini with Sour Cream, Chopped Herring,
and Caviar
Iced Lemon Vodka
Sacher Torte
Hot Tea with Lemon in Glasses

Cold Russian Borscht

4 medium-sized beets
4 cups beef consommé or beef broth
1 medium-sized onion, chopped
½ tsp. salt
½ tsp. pepper
2 tbsp. vinegar
1 cucumber, peeled and diced
½ cup sour cream

1. Steam the whole beets over boiling water for about 15 minutes. Remove them from heat, and save the liquid. Strain the liquid through cheesecloth and pour it into a saucepan. Now peel the beets and discard the skins. (The skins should slip off very easily after steaming, but be careful because they retain their heat a long time.)
2. Grate the peeled beets through the coarsest blade of your grater. Add them to the liquid in the pot. Add beef broth, chopped onion, salt, pepper, and vinegar.
3. Cover. Simmer the soup for 20 minutes over low heat. When ready, chill in refrigerator.

4. Before serving, stir in the diced cucumber and float a big spoonful of sour cream in each soup plate.

Blini with Sour Cream, Chopped Herring, and Caviar

These little pancakes are light as a feather, and combined with the various garnishes, they make a delicious and different meal. The preparation of the batter is done in advance, and as the blini are prepared they should be placed in an ovenproof dish (a round Pyrex pie plate is ideal) resting in a warm oven until all are ready to serve.

BLINI

> *½ envelope dry yeast*
> *4 tbsp. warm water*
> *½ tsp. sugar*
> *1 cup milk*
> *1 cup sifted all-purpose flour*
> *½ tsp. salt*
> *2 eggs, separated*
> *1 cup melted butter*

1. Scald the milk, and then allow it to cool to lukewarm.
2. Soften the yeast in the warm water in a mixing bowl which has previously been warmed. When the yeast is soft, add half the lukewarm milk.
3. Separately, resift the flour with the salt. Now add half the flour to the yeast and milk mixture. Cover the bowl with a cloth and let the batter rise for about ½ hour.
4. Add the rest of the flour and milk, beat the egg yolks separately, and stir them into the mixture. Now stir the whole batter thoroughly until smooth.

5. Cover the bowl again and let the batter rise until it has doubled in size.

6. While the batter is rising, beat the egg whites until they form stiff peaks.

7. When the batter has risen, add the egg whites and 2 tablespoons melted butter, and fold the egg whites into the mixture. Then let it rise for another ½ hour.

8. To bake the blini, heat your griddle or crêpe pan over medium heat. For each blini, pour 1 teaspoon melted butter into the pan, followed by 1 tablespoon batter. Let it cook until broken bubbles show on the top and you can see, by lifting the edge, that the bottom is turning golden brown.

9. Sprinkle a little more melted butter on the uncooked side, then turn and cook for about 30 seconds. Then remove from pan into waiting warmed dish in the oven. This recipe should yield about a dozen blini.

GARNISHES

> *1 cup chopped herring*
> *1 cup sour cream*
> *½ cup melted butter*
> *caviar (red, black, pressed, or beluga, in whatever quantity you can afford and consume!)*

To serve, bring the blini to the table in the warm dish, and the tray of garnishes in attractive bowls with spoons for each. To eat, take one blini at a time, apply melted butter, sour cream, and either herring or caviar, roll up, and eat.

Iced Lemon Vodka

There are many ways to flavor vodka, which is, essentially, a tasteless alcohol. This particular method is simple, but creates a marvelous drink which is also useful in preparing Bloody Marys and martinis, when you're not having a Russian dinner. The one proviso is that it should be done about a month in advance. So right now, while you're thinking about it, follow the instructions.

1 bottle vodka (preferably Polish or Russian, but domestic will do)
1 lemon

1. With a small, sharp paring knife, cut the lemon peel into thin pieces. Avoiding cutting too deeply and picking up any of the inner white, bitter skin.
2. Open the bottle of vodka and slip in the pieces of lemon peel. Close the bottle and store it in your freezer.
3. Remember, the vodka cannot freeze because the freezing point of alcohol is a much lower temperature than that of your refrigerator freezing compartment. Over a period of weeks the vodka will turn a golden yellow as the lemon oil is absorbed from the peel into the liquid. It will have a gentle lemon flavor and will require no additional ice when served directly from the bottle in a small stemmed glass. For martinis, this method eliminates the need of using ice or lemon peel. You simply pour the iced vodka into a chilled martini glass, stir in a few drops of vermouth, and a perfect vodka martini is yours. For a Bloody Mary, simply omit the lemon from your regular ingredients.

Sacher Torte

This is a one-layer cake with icing. You should use a 9-inch cake pan, 3 inches deep.

CAKE

> ½ cup melted butter
> 5 eggs, separated
> ½ cup sugar
> ¼ cup cocoa powder
> ½ cup sifted flour

1. Beat the melted butter and the egg yolks together thoroughly in a bowl.
2. Preheat oven to 250 degrees.
3. Add the sugar, cocoa, and flour to the mixture, and beat until smooth.
4. Separately, beat the egg whites with an electric mixer or hand beater until stiff.
5. Fold the egg whites into the flour mixture, pour into lightly oiled cake pan, and bake in preheated oven for 1 hour. Test for doneness by inserting a cake needle into the center of the cake. If cooked, it should come out clean. When ready, slip a knife around the edge of the cake pan and turn out onto a cooling rack.

ICING

> 4 egg whites
> 1½ cups powdered (confectioners') sugar
> 1 tbsp. lemon juice

1. Beat all the ingredients together with an electric beater or hand beater at slow speed until smooth.
2. Spread the icing over top and sides of cooled cake with flexible spatula. This cake does not need to be refrigerated until use, because of the egg-white base of the icing.

~♦~

DINNER X
Baked Manicotti
Artichoke, Olive, and Lettuce Salad
Cannoli
Red Chianti
Cafe Espresso

~♦~

Baked Manicotti

This dish is composed of three elements—the meat sauce, the pasta, and the filling. I present each as a separate operation, with directions for assemblisg the manicotti at the very end. I know this looks like a long recipe, but it's well worth the effort and the time. The proportions given here yield generous servings for two. But if you want to make more, you can confidently double, or even triple, the recipe quantities.

MEAT SAUCE

> *3 strips bacon, cut into 1-inch pieces*
> *2 tbsp. olive oil*
> *2 tbsp. butter*
> *½ cup chopped onions*
> *½ lb. ground beef*
> *¼ lb. ground pork (shoulder)*
> *¼ lb. ground calves liver*
> *2 cloves garlic, peeled and crushed*
> *1 bay leaf*
> *½ tsp. black pepper*
> *3 large ripe fresh tomatoes, diced*
> *1 stalk celery, finely minced*
> *1 6-oz. can tomato paste*
> *1 tsp. salt*

1. Using a medium-sized saucepan, heat together the butter, olive oil, and bacon.
2. Now add the onions and cook for 5 minutes over medium heat until they just begin to color.
3. Add the beef, pork and liver, garlic, bay leaf, and pepper and cook over low heat for 20 minutes, stirring occasionally.
4. Now add remaining ingredients and cook, covered, for 2 hours over low heat, just barely bubbling. Stir occasionally, and make sure tomatoes get well mixed with the rest of the sauce as their shapes disintegrate from the cooking.
5. When the sauce is ready, set it aside, away from heat, to await final assembly.

FILLING

½ *cup ricotta cheese*
½ *cup mozzarella cheese, cut into small pieces*
1 *egg*
½ *cup Swiss cheese, grated*
2 *tbsp. butter*
5 *tbsp. grated Parmesan cheese*
¼ *tsp. black pepper*

Combine all the ingredients in a bowl, mix thoroughly, and set aside for final assembly.

PASTA

1½ *cups sifted flour*
2 *eggs*
¼ *tsp. salt*
2 *tbsp. cold water*
1 *tbsp. olive oil*
4 *tbsp. grated Parmesan cheese*

1. In a bowl, mix the flour, eggs, and water to make a thick dough. Then move the dough to a lightly floured board, and knead it thoroughly for about 5 minutes until it feels springy. Then let it set for about 1 hour, covered with a piece of damp cheesecloth.
2. Cut the dough in half, and roll out each half as thinly as possible. When rolled out, cut into roughly 6-inch squares. This should yield 6 or 8 pieces, depending on thickness.
3. Using your biggest pot, bring several quarts of water to a boil, adding to it, the salt and the olive oil. Drop the pieces of pasta into the water and cook at full boil

for 6 minutes. Remove from water and dry on paper towels.

FINAL ASSEMBLY

1. Divide the filling into as many equal amounts as you have pieces of pasta.

2. Using a rectangular Pyrex baking pan large enough to comfortably hold all the manicotti, spoon enough meat sauce in the bottom of the pan to make it about ¼ inch deep. Then put the proper amount of stiffing on each piece of pasta, spread it evenly, roll up the pasta, and place the roll in the baking pan, parallel to the short side, seam-side down. Repeat this process until all the rolls are in the pan, side by side, with a little space in between. Pour the rest of the meat sauce over the top and sprinkle with the remaining Parmesan.

3. Bake at 325 degrees for 15 minutes, and serve immediately. It is best to bring the Pyrex dish directly to the table and place on a trivet. It is not necessary to use heated plates because the manicotti will be very hot.

Artichoke, Olive, and Lettuce Salad

6 artichoke hearts
1 small head lettuce
1 doz. large pitted black olives
2 tbsp. olive oil
1 tbsp. vinegar
½ tsp. salt
¼ tsp. pepper

1. Mix the oil, vinegar, salt, and pepper together in a salad bowl.

2. Wash and drain the lettuce, tearing the leaves into 1½-inch pieces.

3. Drain the artichoke hearts and cut them in half.

4. Cut the olives in half.

5. Add the salad ingredients to the dressing in the bowl, toss, and serve.

Cannoli

You may not recognize the name, but when you see the results of this recipe you will be agreeably surprised. To make the cannoli properly, you will need two or three pieces of wood about 6 inches long and about 1 inch in diameter. I suggest sanding down an old broom handle. Make sure the paint is completely removed and the finish is smooth. Then cut into 6-inch lengths, rub with oil, wrap in paper, and put away until use.

3 tbsp. powdered (confectioners') sugar
1 tbsp. butter
1 egg
½ cup flour
1 tbsp. sherry
¼ lb. ricotta cheese, drained
½ tsp. vanilla extract
1 tbsp. heavy cream
oil for deep frying

1. To form the dough, mix together the first five ingredients, using 1 tablespoon of the sugar. If too loose, add a little flour; if too stiff, add a little water. Separate into pieces about the equivalent of a sphere 1 inch in diameter. On a lightly floured board, roll each ball of dough out into an oval shape about ⅛ inch thick. Now wrap

around one of the pieces of wood described above, and seal edge.

2. In your deep fryer, heat the oil to 350 degrees.

3. Slip one piece of dough at a time from the wood and into the oil. Fry each one golden brown before carefully removing and cooking next one. Drain the ready cannoli cones on paper towels and allow them to cool.

4. Beat the remaining ingredients together, using the rest of the sugar, to form a smooth cream. Fill the cones with cream and refrigerate until time to serve.

DINNER XI

Bacon-Wrapped Trout
Boiled Parsley Potatoes
Buttered Steamed Zucchini
Fresh Blueberry Tart
White Wine

Bacon-Wrapped Trout

Although freshly caught brook trout has no peer, I have seen freshly frozen Colorado trout in various supermarkets. It is as close as you can come to the real thing without actually wetting a line. If you use frozen trout for this recipe, make sure to let it thaw out completely at room temperature before using.

2 *fresh or frozen trout, cleaned*
4 *strips hickory-smoked bacon*
2 *tbsp. chopped onions*
2 *tbsp. butter*
½ *tsp. pepper*

1. Stuff each trout with the chopped onions and 1 table-spoon butter cut into small pieces.
2. Now wrap each trout with 2 strips of bacon and secure with toothpicks.
3. Sprinkle the trout with pepper and broil each side under medium heat for about 10 minutes.
4. To serve, transfer to hot serving platter. Add lemon wedges and a sprinkle of chopped parsley.

Boiled Parsley Potatoes

2 *large potatoes, peeled and cut in half*
2 *tbsp. butter*
1 *tbsp. chopped parsley*

1. Boil the potatoes in slightly salted water until they are tender (about 15 to 20 minutes). They are ready when a fork will go into one with little effort, but without causing the potato to fall apart.
2. Transfer the potatoes to a warm serving dish, add the butter and sprinkle with parsley.
3. Toss the potatoes lightly until the butter is mostly melted and the parsley is well distributed. Keep warm until time to serve.

Buttered Steamed Zucchini

2 *medium-sized zucchini*
2 *tbsp. butter*
½ *tsp. salt*

1. Wash thoroughly, but do not peel the zucchini.
2. Steam the zucchini over boiling water on a steaming platform for 20 minutes.
3. To serve, split each zucchini in half lengthwise, add the butter, sprinkle with salt, and serve piping hot.

Fresh Blueberry Tart

Follow the directions for the Raspberry Tart in Lunch III, page 48, substituting 1½ cups fresh, washed and drained blueberries for the raspberries.

DINNER XII

Avocado Stuffed with Crabmeat
Roast Young Chicken with Herb Stuffing
Creamed Chopped Spinach
Hot Green Apple Pie with Cheddar Cheese
Red Wine

Avocado Stuffed with Crabmeat

1 *large ripe bit firm avocado*
1 *cup cooked fresh crabmeat*
¾ *cup mayonnaise*
2 *tbsp. tomato paste*
1 *tsp. dill (minced fresh, or dried dillweed)*
½ *tsp. salt*
¼ *tsp. pepper*
2 *hard-cooked eggs*

1. Cut the avocado in half lengthwise and remove the pit.

Cut a thin slice from the skin on the underside of each half to allow the halves to sit without rolling.

2. Stuff the cavities full of crabmeat, so that it makes a mound over the whole flat surface of the avocado halves.

3. In a bowl, mix the mayonnaise, tomato paste, dill, salt, and pepper thoroughly.

4. Separate the yolks from the whites of the hard-cooked eggs.

5. Rub the whites through a sieve into the mayonnaise mixture in the bowl.

6. Mix well, then generously spoon the sauce over the crabmeat and avocado.

7. Now rub the hard-cooked yolks through the sieve over the sauce for garnish. Refrigerate (but not too long) until serving.

Roast Young Chicken with Herb Stuffing

STUFFING

> *1 medium-sized onion*
> *2 stalks celery*
> *3 cups dry breadcrumbs*
> *¼ lb. butter*
> *½ tsp. salt*
> *½ tsp. freshly ground pepper*
> *1 tsp. dried thyme leaves*
> *1 cup chicken broth*
> *liver from the chicken*

1. In a medium-sized enameled saucepan, melt half the butter in 1 cup of chicken broth over medium heat.

2. While the butter is melting, preheat oven to 350 degrees.

3. Chop the celery and onion very finely, and simmer in the remaining butter in a skillet over medium heat.

4. Take the raw chicken liver and liquefy it, either in a blender or by chopping so finely that it becomes liquid.

5. Now to assemble the stuffing, drop the breadcrumbs into the melted butter and chicken broth, stirring well. Then stir in the softened onions and celery, and finally the raw chicken liver. As you stir in the liver, you will see that it changes from the deep brownish-red color into pinkish grey because it is cooking from contact with the hot ingredients. The remainder of this cooking process takes place inside the chicken while it is roasting.

6. Stir the thyme leaves, salt, and pepper into the stuffing and remove from heat.

CHICKEN

> 1 young fryer chicken (4 or 5 lbs. with giblets)
> ½ tsp. salt
> ¼ tsp. pepper
> 1 cup chicken broth
> 4 tbsp. butter
> 1 strip bacon
> ¼ tsp. poultry seasoning

1. Take the chicken and dry it thoroughly inside and out with paper towels. Salt and pepper the cavity, then spoon in the stuffing. When full, truss the chicken. Butter the outside skin and sprinkle with poultry seasoning.

2. Cut the strip of bacon in half lengthwise and lay one half on top of the breast on each side of the breastbone.

3. Place the chicken on a roasting rack in a shallow roasting pan and place in preheated oven. Set timer to

provide 25 minutes' roasting time per pound (1 hour and 40 minutes for a 4-pound chicken).

4. When the chicken is in the oven, put the cup of chicken broth in a small saucepan on the stove over very low heat. Add to it the giblets, heart, and neck of the chicken and let it simmer very gently while the chicken roasts. This broth will be used for basting, if necessary, and later, to make the gravy.

5. Not much basting is required for the first ½ hour or so, but thereafter the chicken should be basted thoroughly every 10 minutes for the remainder of the cooking time. This is the secret of making roast chicken so that it is moist and tender, and never dry. If there are not enough drippings in the bottom of the pan to baste with, add a little broth from the stove to the pan, then baste with it after it has mixed with the drippings. The best way is to use a basting bulb. It works faster than a spoon and therefore reduces the time the oven door must be kept open. When the time is up, the chicken should be golden brown, the skin crisp, the meat moist and tender, but cooked through. To check, make a cut under the joint of one of the legs. The dark meat near the bone should not look bloody. If it does, cook 10 or 15 minutes longer and look again.

6. To serve, quickly transfer the cooked chicken to the carving board or serving platter. Then quickly remove the giblets from the broth, chop finely, and put them in the roasting pan, along with the remaining extra broth. Hold the roasting pan over a burner on the stove and quickly bring to a boil. Scrape up all the drippings so that they blend into the liquid. You may add a little wine —any kind you have open—for added taste. Transfer the hot gravy to a gravy boat.

7. Take the chicken into the dining room and carve quickly, and serve with the stuffing and hot gravy.

§ NOTE: If you do this right, it is one of the most simple and delicious dishes in the world. I personally test restaurants by ordering roast chicken. If it is good, everything else seems to turn out well, but if it is served tough and dry, with limp skin and insufficient or floury gravy, then I can usually count on lackluster performance in every other department as well!

Creamed Chopped Spinach

1 lb. fresh spinach leaves
2 tbsp. butter
1 tsp. salt
½ tsp. Maggi seasoning
1 tsp. vinegar
½ cup heavy cream

1. Wash the spinach leaves thoroughly under cold water and cut away the thick stalks.
2. In a large saucepan, bring 3 or 4 qts. of water to a rolling boil, add salt, drop in the spinach leaves.
3. Boil for 10 minutes.
4. Drain leaves. On a board, chop the spinach very finely.
5. Melt the butter over low heat in a medium-sized saucepan, stir in the chopped spinach, then the vinegar and the Maggi seasoning.
6. Finally, add the heavy cream and leave over low heat another 2 or 3 minutes until heated through but not boiling. Keep warm until serving time. Be careful not to allow spinach to boil because that can curdle the cream.

Hot Green Apple Pie with Cheddar Cheese

CRUST

> 1 *cup sifted flour*
> ½ *tsp. salt*
> 4 *tbsp. vegetable shortening*
> 3 *tbsp. cold water*
> 1 *tsp. sugar*

1. Mix the flour, sugar, and salt in a bowl. Then cut the shortening into the dry ingredients and mix until they have the appearance of corn flakes.

2. Now sprinkle water, a little at a time, over the dough, stirring continually.

3. Finally, gather the dough into a mass, knead slightly, and form into a ball.

4. On a lightly floured board, roll out dough to approximately a 12-inch circle (for an 8-inch pan). Fold it over once, place it in the pie pan, then unfold. Smooth out any bumps, then trim edges. Now crimp edges to the edges of the pan with pressure from the tines of an ordinary fork. The pie is now ready for filling.

5. Preheat oven to 425 degrees.

FILLING

> 1 *cup sugar*
> 2 *tbsp. flour*
> 4 *tbsp. Sultana raisins*
> 1 *tbsp. grated orange rind*
> 1 *tsp. cinnamon*
> ¼ *tsp. ground nutmeg*
> ½ *tsp. salt*
> 6 *cups peeled, cored, and sliced green apples*
> 2 *tbsp. butter*
> 4 *wedges sharp cheddar cheese (to serve along with the pie)*

1. Toss all ingredients, except butter and cheese, together in a bowl.

2. Fill pastry-lined pan, then dot the surface of the filling with butter. Bake in middle level of preheated oven for 45 minutes. Serve hot with the wedges of cheddar cheese.

❦

DINNER XIII

Soused (Marinated) Shrimp Cocktail
Steak au Poivre
French Fried Onion Rings
Beefsteak Tomato and Onion Salad
Individual Chocolate Soufflés
Vintage Burgundy

❦

Soused (Marinated) Shrimp Cocktail

½ *lb. cooked fresh shrimps*
1 *cup olive oil*
¼ *cup lemon juice*
1 *tbsp. chopped parsley*
2 *cloves garlic, very finely minced*
10 *cracked black peppercorns*
1 *bay leaf*
½ *tsp. salt*

1. Mix all the ingredients, except the shrimps, in a shallow bowl.
2. Add the cooked shrimps to the mixture and make sure they are covered with liquid. If they are not, you will either have to find a different container or turn them periodically.
3. Refrigerate several hours, preferably overnight.
4. To serve, divide the shrimp into two portions, arrange attractively on plates, and serve with a small bowl of the marinade for dipping. Garnish with a sprig of parsley and a lemon wedge.

Steak au Poivre

2 one-half lb. sirloin steaks, trimmed of fat and bone
1 tbsp. peppercorns, crushed but not ground
2 tbsp. butter
¼ cup red wine
¼ cup beef consommé

1. Spread the peppercorns on a piece of paper towel.
2. Press the steaks down on the peppercorns on both sides, so that the pepper clings to the surface of the steaks.
3. In a cast iron skillet, melt the butter and fry the steaks in it over medium heat. For 1-inch steaks, about 5 minutes each side for rare, 8 minutes each side for medium. I don't want to discuss "well done," because you shouldn't be eating steaks prepared this way if you like them overcooked.
4. When the steaks are ready, remove them from the pan to warm dinner plates or a serving platter.
5. Add the wine and the consommé to the pan, bring to a quick boil, and reduce volume of liquid by one half. Pour half the resulting sauce over each steak and serve immediately.

French Fried Onion Rings

2 medium-sized onions, peeled and sliced into rings
4 cups cooking oil
1 cup flour

1. Separate the onion rings from each other.
2. Put the flour into a paper or plastic bag, followed by the onion rings.
3. Heat cooking oil to 375 degrees in deep fryer.

4. Hold bag so as to seal it, and shake it well to coat the onions with the flour.

5. Fry the floured onion rings in the oil until golden. Remove with fryer basket or tongs, drain on paper towel, and serve with the steaks.

Beefsteak Tomato and Onion Salad

1 medium-sized Bermuda onion
4 tbsp. olive oil
2 tbsp. vinegar
1 large firm beefsteak tomato
½ tsp. pepper
1 tbsp. chopped fresh chives

1. Well in advance, peel and slice the onion into very thin slices. Lay them flat in a shallow container such as a Pyrex baking dish. Pour over the oil and vinegar and let them marinate for a minimum of 2 hours.

2. Just before dinner, slice the tomato into a salad bowl. Add the marinated onions with all the liquid. Add seasonings, sprinkle with the chives, toss lightly, and serve.

Individual Chocolate Soufflés

For this recipe you will need to have two small soufflé dishes. These are made of oven-proof white pottery, with about a 1½-cup capacity. They are round, and the outside is usually decoratively fluted in a vertical pattern. Any dish of the same capacity would be acceptable, but the ones I've described are particularly appropriate because they are attractive enough to serve at the table for an elegant meal.

The soufflé takes about 20 minutes to bake. It is very delicate and must be removed from the oven and served immediately when *it* is damned good and ready. So carefully plan your meal to have all the previous courses finished when the dessert is ready. It is better to finish early and wait a few minutes for the soufflé. Even a minute's delay in serving can cause it to collapse and be ruined. One rule I always observe is to have a standby dessert ready when I plan to serve soufflé to guests for dessert—just in case of disaster. Also, I try not to make any announcements about the soufflé before it arrives in the dining room at the peak of its glory. What the guests never knew cannot disappoint them!

> *2 tbsp. soft butter*
> *1 tbsp. cake flour*
> *2 oz. cooking chocolate*
> *1½ tbsp. corn starch*
> *½ cup milk*
> *4 tbsp. sugar*
> *3 eggs, separated*
> *¼ tsp. salt*
> *2 tbsp. powdered (confectioners') sugar*

1. Preheat oven to 375 degrees.
2. Butter the insides of the soufflé dishes, bottom and sides, then swish the cake flour around in them. Knock out any flour that doesn't adhere.
3. Melt the chocolate over simmering water in a double boiler, adding about 1 tablespoon water to it. Keep it warm but do not allow the water underneath to boil.
4. Mix the cornstarch, milk, and 3 tablespoons of sugar together in a saucepan until smooth. Bring to a boil,

remove from heat immediately, then stir the chocolate into the mixture.

5. Add the remaining butter to the mixture without mixing it in. Allow to cool.

6. With an electric or hand beater, beat the whites of the three eggs and the salt together until soft peaks are formed, then add the remaining 1 tablespoon of sugar and continue beating until stiff.

7. In a mixing bowl, mix two egg yolks with the cooled chocolate sauce. Then fold the egg whites into the sauce.

8. Carefully pour, with the help of a rubber scraper, the chocolate soufflé batter into the two soufflé dishes (1 inch from the top edge).

9. Bake about 20 minutes in the preheated oven. Do not open oven door to look. It is best to have an oven with a glass door so that you can see what is happening. When the soufflé rises about 2 or more inches above the rims of the dishes, it is ready. Sprinkle the top with the powdered sugar and serve immediately.

DINNER XIV

Chicken Liver Crêpes
French-Cut String Beans
Caesar Salad
Lemon Sherbet Meringues
Iced Tea Punch

Chicken Liver Crepes

CRÊPES

> *1 tbsp. melted butter*
> *¾ cup sifted flour*
> *¼ tsp. salt*
> *2 eggs*
> *1 cup milk*
> *shortening or butter for cooking*

1. Mix the first 5 ingredients with an egg beater until smooth and well blended.

2. For each crêpe, using an 8- or 9-inch crêpe pan or skillet, melt 1 teaspoon butter or shortening. Using a ladle, pour about 4 tablespoons batter into the pan, then rotate the pan in a quick motion to spread batter evenly over entire cooking surface before it sets.

3. Cook over medium heat until the edges brown and pull away slightly from the cooking surface.

4. With a long, flat spatula flip the crêpe over and cook the other side for a few seconds.

5. Flip crêpe out of the pan into an ovenproof Pyrex

dish kept warm in the oven. Continue until all the crêpes are done.

FILLING

> ½ *lb. fresh chicken livers*
> 2 *tbsp. butter*
> ½ *tsp. salt*
> ¼ *cup white wine*
> 1 *tbsp. Worcestershire sauce*

1. Cut the chicken livers apart, remove the tendons, and then cut each separate liver in half.
2. Melt the butter in a skillet, fry the livers for about 5 minutes, turning to make sure all sides get browned equally.
3. Lower heat, sprinkle on the salt, add the wine and the Worcestershire sauce to the pan and simmer another 2 minutes.
4. Just before serving, quickly remove crêpes from the dish in the oven, one at a time. Lay the crêpe out on a board and spoon about 4 tablespoons of the chicken livers onto it. Include a little sauce to keep the filling moist. Roll each crêpe around the livers, tucking the ends under, and transfer to warm serving platter or dinner plates. When the crêpes are filled, add any leftover sauce with livers over the top, and serve hot.

French-Cut String Beans

The most important piece of equipment needed to make these beans come out perfectly is a string bean cutter. It is often found as an extra feature on the handle end of a potato peeler. The string bean cutter is merely a little square aperture just about big enough for a bean to fit through it. Three or four razor-sharp blades are set into the opening, parallel to each other. You push the end of the string bean into the opening against the sharp edges of the blades. Then you grasp the emerging piece of the bean on the other side and pull it through to complete the cut. The string bean has been sliced lengthwise into three or four parts.

1 lb. fresh string beans
1 tbsp. butter
¼ tsp. salt
¼ tsp. pepper
1 tbsp. Maggi seasoning

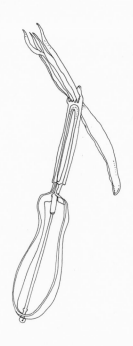

1. Wash the string beans, then snip off both ends of each bean, and pass through the cutter.

2. Steam the beans over boiling water on a steaming platform for about 8 minutes.

3. Transfer immediately to warmed serving dish, sprinkle with salt and pepper, add piece of butter and Maggi seasoning. Cover with cloth napkin to keep warm, and serve.

Caesar Salad

1 head romaine lettuce
1 small clove garlic
½ tsp. salt
½ tsp. English mustard
1 tsp. lemon juice
4 drops Tabasco sauce
2 tbsp. olive oil
4 anchovy fillets
1 raw egg
½ cup croutons (packaged, or diced stale bread which has been slightly browned in the broiler)
1 tbsp. grated Parmesan cheese

1. Separate the leaves of romaine and wash. Set in colander to drain.

2. Peel the garlic clove. In a wooden salad bowl crush the garlic with the salt using the back of a wooden spoon. Then add the mustard, Tabasco, lemon juice, and olive oil. Mix thoroughly.

3. Tear the lettuce leaves into the salad bowl, add the croutons, anchovies, and Parmesan, then break the egg into the salad.

4. Finally, toss very thoroughly so that the egg gets well

blended and the croutons soak up some oil and garlic, and the cheese is well distributed throughout.

Lemon Sherbet Meringues

2 egg whites
⅛ tsp. cream of tartar
⅛ tsp. salt
½ cup sugar
½ tsp. vanilla extract
2 scoops lemon (or other flavor) sherbet
butter and flour to prepare cookie sheet

1. Butter one cookie sheet, then lightly sprinkle with flour. Knock off any excess flour that doesn't adhere to the butter.
2. Preheat oven to 200 degrees.
3. Mix the egg whites, vanilla, cream of tartar, and salt in a bowl.
4. Now beat the mixture until it forms soft peaks. Continue beating, adding the sugar, 1 spoonful at a time, until all the sugar is absorbed.
5. Using a large cooking spoon, spoon the mixture onto the cookie sheet in semicircular-shaped portions at least 2 inches apart.
6. Turn off the oven. Place the cookie sheet at the middle level and leave for at least 4 hours, or overnight. This permits the meringues to dry rather than cook, and the result is far superior.
7. To serve, arrange a meringue on each side of a scoop of sherbet in a dessert saucer. Another way to serve is to put one meringue on the bottom, add a scoop of sherbet, and put the other meringue on top of the sherbet, like a sandwich.

Iced Tea Punch

1 qt. freshly made strong tea
¼ cup fresh lime juice
1 thinly sliced fresh lime
½ cup honey (clear liquid type)
½ cup rum

1. Put half the tea, the lime juice, honey, and rum into a blender. Run at medium speed for 1 minute.
2. Pour the mixture into a large pitcher, add the remaining tea and the sliced lime. Fill the pitcher with ice cubes and keep in refrigerator until time to pour.

DINNER XV

Tequila Margueritas
Guacamole with Corn Chips
Chicken and Beef Tacos
Refried Beans
Cold Guavas with Cream Cheese

Tequila Margueritas

ONE COCKTAIL

1 oz. 90-proof tequila
½ oz. triple sec or cointreau
1 tbsp. fresh lime juice
1 dash orange bitters
1 tsp. superfine granulated bar sugar
salt

1. Wet the rim of a standard cocktail glass and dip it in salt so that the whole rim is coated with about ⅛ inch of salt.

2. In a shaker with ice, combine all the other ingredients and shake vigorously.

3. Pour through strainer and serve immediately.

Guacamole with Corn Chips

> *1 large ripe avocado*
> *1 tbsp. finely minced onion*
> *1 tsp. lime juice*
> *2 cloves garlic, finely minced*
> *5 drops Tabasco sauce or similar hot sauce*

1. Peel and pit the avocado.

2. Crush the garlic, onions, and salt together in a bowl.

3. Add the remaining ingredients and mash together with a fork. Then stir to assure even distribution of seasonings.

4. Serve with corn chips as a dip to accompany tequila margueritas.

§ NOTE: Do not let the guacamole sit around too long before serving as the avocado has a tendency to discolor.

Chicken and Beef Tacos

Tacos are tortillas filled with various fillings, fried, and then served hot. What follows is the recipe for making the tortillas, then the two different fillings. The recipe will yield six tortillas. The fillings are enough for three tacos each. If you prefer one filling to the other, you may adjust the quantities accordingly. Just keep in mind that three tacos are plenty for one person.

TORTILLAS

> *2 cups regular flour*
> *1 tsp. salt*
> *¼ cup vegetable shortening*
> *½ cup water*

1. Sift the flour and salt together into a bowl. Cut the shortening into the dry ingredients.
2. Add the water, and knead thoroughly until you have a smooth dough that holds together.
3. Now divide dough into 6 equal pieces and roll each one into a ball. Cover the balls with a damp cloth and let stand 20 minutes.
4. On a lightly floured board, roll each ball into an 8-inch round pancake.
5. Heat a medium-sized skillet and fry the tortillas, one at a time, without adding any shortening to the skillet. Turn them once, cooking both sides until golden brown.
6. Set the cooked tortillas aside until ready to fill. Keep in mind that they will eventually harden and will need to be heated again to allow filling and rolling. So the faster you work, the better.

CHICKEN FILLING

> *1 tbsp. butter*
> *½ cup chopped onion*
> *1 medium-sized tomato, chopped*
> *¼ cup chopped green pepper*
> *1 cup cubed cooked chicken*
> *½ tsp. salt*

Soften the onion in the butter over low heat in a skillet. Add the tomatoes and peppers and cook a few minutes more. Then add the chicken, stir well, and continue cooking for about 5 minutes. Filling is ready.

BEEF FILLING

> *1 tbsp. olive oil*
> *½ cup chopped onion*
> *½ lb. ground beef*
> *¼ cup chopped green pepper*
> *1 small clove garlic, peeled and crushed*
> *1 medium-sized tomato, chopped*
> *½ tsp. salt*

Soften the onion in the olive oil over low heat in a skillet. Add the meat, turn up heat, and brown. Now add remaining ingredients and cook for about 5 minutes, stirring occasionally. Filling is ready.

FINAL ASSEMBLY

> *¼ cup olive oil for frying*
> *½ head iceberg lettuce, shredded*

1. Fill and roll three tortillas with the chicken filling, three with the beef. (If the tortillas sat a long time after preparation. it may be necessary to warm them in the oven before attempting to roll them.)
2. Fry the filled tortillas on both sides in the oil until very hot, but not burning or smoking.
3. Serve the tacos on a bed of shredded lettuce.

Refried Beans

½ lb. dried red beans
1 qt. water
2 tsp. salt
4 tbsp. bacon fat or lard
½ cup sour cream
1 tbsp. finely chopped scallions

1. Cook the beans in the salted water over low heat for several hours until they are very tender.
2. When done, drain off any water remaining (there should be hardly any).
3. Separately, melt the fat without allowing it to burn.
4. Using a potato masher, mash the beans until you have a smooth purée, then stir in the fat, a little at a time, until all is absorbed.
5. Now heat a little more fat in a frying pan, add the beans, and cook over medium heat, continually stirring until the beans are dry.
6. Mix the sour cream and chopped scallions together in a small bowl. Serve the refried beans topped with a spoonful of the sour cream mixture on each portion.

Cold Guavas with Cream Cheese

It is practically impossible to find fresh guavas in the United States, so this recipe calls for the use of canned guavas. It is a particularly appropriate dessert with this meal.

1 can guavas containing at least 4 halves
1 4-oz. package cream cheese

1. Arrange 2 guava halves in each of 2 dessert saucers.
2. Now divide the cream cheese into 2 equal portions and add it to the plates. Serve.

DINNER XVI

Artichoke Bottoms Stuffed with
Anchovy Sour Cream
Roast Duckling with Apple Stuffing
German-Style Red Cabbage
Light Green Salad with Lemon Dressing
Coffee Custard with Gooseberry Preserves
Red Wine

Artichoke Bottoms Stuffed with
Anchovy Sour Cream

2 large artichokes
1 tbsp. olive oil
1 clove garlic, cut into 4 pieces
5 cracked peppercorns
2 tbsp. vinegar
½ cup sour cream
1 tsp. anchovy paste

1. Steam the artichokes over boiling water containing the olive oil, garlic, peppercorns, and vinegar for 25 minutes.
2. Remove from heat and let the artichokes cool before handling them.
3. When they are cool, pick off all the leaves. Then with a small sharp knife, cut away the small pieces of artichoke clinging to the bases of the leaves and save. Discard the leaves.
4. Remove the choke from the artichoke bottoms. Now refrigerate the bottoms until ready to serve.
5. In a small bowl, mix the sour cream, anchovy paste, and the small bits of artichoke cut from the leaves. Refrigerate until ready to serve.
6. To serve, spoon half the sour cream mixture into the cup of each artichoke bottom. Garnish each with a lemon wedge and serve.

Roast Duckling with Apple Stuffing

STUFFING

½ cup chopped onions
¼ lb. butter
4 cups stale bread cubes or soft breadcrumbs
1 raw duck liver, minced
2 tbsp. chopped parsley
2 cups peeled apples, cut into ½-inch pieces
½ cup white raisins
½ cup chicken or beef consommé

1. Melt the butter and soften the onions in it in a large saucepan. Add the breadcrumbs and brown them lightly.

2. Add the rest of the ingredients, toss well and heat through, then remove from heat.

DUCKLING

> 1 *young duckling (about 4 lbs.)*
> 1 *tsp. salt*
> 1 *cup chicken or beef consommé*

1. Preheat oven to 325 degrees.
2. Wash the duck in cold water and dry thoroughly inside and out.
3. Sprinkle the cavity with salt, then fill with the stuffing prepared earlier.
4. Truss the duck and place it on a rack in preheated oven.
5. Prick duck in fatty areas to allow fat to drain out during the roasting.
6. Roast for 1½ hours, frequently removing the accumulated fat in the pan with a basting bulb.
7. When cooked, remove the duck and the rack from the roasting pan and place duck on warmed serving platter.
8. Skim as much fat as possible off the juices in the roasting pan. Add the consommé and the giblets of the duck to roasting pan and simmer over high heat until volume is reduced by one-half. Remove giblets, pour sauce into gravy boat and serve with duck.
9. The easiest way to serve the duck for two is simply to remove the stuffing with a large spoon, divide the duck in half with a sharp carving knife, and serve each person half the duck and half the stuffing.

German-Style Red Cabbage

2 *cups shredded red cabbage*
½ *medium-sized tart apple, peeled and thinly sliced*
½ *cup thinly sliced onion*
2 *tbsp. vinegar*
2 *tbsp. butter*
2 *tbsp. sugar*
¼ *cup red wine*
1 *tsp. arrowroot*

1. In a medium-sized skillet, melt the butter over medium heat. Add the sliced apples and onions and cook until the onion is transparent but not browned. Then stir in the shredded cabbage, followed by the sugar and the wine.

2. Cover the pan and cook over medium low heat for 5 minutes, stirring occasionally. Do not allow any burning—if your skillet has "hot spots," stir more frequently and use a lower heat.

3. When the cabbage is tender, separately mix the arrowroot with a large spoonful of the liquid from the pan until the arrowroot is completely dissolved. Then stir it back into the cabbage and allow the whole thing to cook 2 or 3 minutes longer. Keep warm until ready to serve.

Light Green Salad with Lemon Dressing

For this heavy meal, a light salad is in order. Use only the youngest light green bibb lettuce, fresh chives, and fresh watercress.

1 *small head bibb lettuce*
1 *bunch watercress, stalks trimmed*
1 *tbsp. olive oil*
1 *tbsp. lemon juice*
2 *tbsp. freshly chopped chives*
½ *tsp. salt*
¼ *tsp. pepper*
½ *tsp. granulated sugar*

1. Wash and drain the lettuce and the watercress.
2. In a salad bowl, mix all the remaining ingredients thoroughly to make the dressing.
3. Tear the lettuce leaves into the bowl in 1½-inch pieces, add watercress, toss, and serve.

Coffee Custard with Gooseberry Preserves

½ *cup strong coffee, preferably espresso*
¾ *cup milk*
4 *tbsp. sugar*
2 *egg yolks*
gooseberry preserves

1. Put the first 4 ingredients in a blender jar and blend for 15 seconds.
2. Transfer mixture into individual custard cups (two large ones).
3. Preheat oven to 325 degrees.
4. Put about 1 inch of hot water into a baking pan. Set the filled custard cups in the water and carefully put the pan in the oven. Bake 40 minutes.
5. Remove the custard cups from the water and place on a rack to cool. The custard may be served at room temperature in the cups, or (better) chilled in the

refrigerator, unmolded, and served on a dessert dish garnished with the gooseberry preserves.

§ WARNING: Do not put the very hot custard cups directly into the refrigerator from the oven. First allow them to cool to room temperature.

❧

DINNER XVII

Sorrel Soup Garnished with Hard-Cooked
Egg Half
Sautéed Calves Liver and Bacon
Puréed Potatoes
Salade Russe
Vanilla-Rum Custard
Red Wine

❧

Sorrel Soup

1-pint jar preserved sorrel
1½ cups concentrated beef consommé
1 cup (½ pt.) heavy cream
1 egg

1. Combine the sorrel and the beef consommé in a saucepan and heat to a simmer. Reduce heat and keep hot but not boiling.
2. Beat the heavy cream until it forms soft peaks. Hard-cook the egg, peel, and cut it in half.
3. Stir the whipped cream into the soup and continue to heat over low heat, not allowing it to boil. Heat through.

4. To serve, ladle into soup dishes and garnish each serving by floating half a hard-cooked egg in the soup.

Sautéed Calves Liver and Bacon

The most important element in making this dinner taste good is the quality and the thinness of the liver. Make sure your butcher provides you with the freshest and youngest calves liver, and that it is sliced no more than ¼ inch thick.

4 thin slices calves liver
4 strips hickory-smoked bacon
3 tbsp. flour
1 tbsp. olive oil
1 tbsp. butter

1. Fry the bacon until crisp, drain on a paper towel, and set aside.
2. In a large cast iron skillet, melt the butter in the olive oil and bring to a sizzle.
3. While the oil and butter are heating, dust each slice of liver with flour, making sure it is completely coated. This should be a dusting, not a thick layer.
4. When the oil and butter are sizzling, put in the liver and sauté for 2 minutes or less on each side. Remove from heat and serve immediately, flanked by the bacon.

Puréed Potatoes

4 medium-sized potatoes, peeled and cut in half
2 tbsp. butter
½ cup sour cream
1 tsp. salt

1. Boil the potatoes in salted water until they are tender.
2. Quickly drain off the water, leaving the potatoes in the pot.
3. Add the remaining ingredients and vigorously mash the potatoes with a potato masher until they are quite smooth. It is important to do this quickly so that they don't cool down too much.
4. Keep warm on an electric warming tray until serving time.

§ OPTIONAL: After mashing potatoes, add 1 tablespoon finely minced onions, and stir. The onions cook a bit from the heat of the surrounding potatoes and yield an interesting extra flavor.

Salade Russe

The vegetables used in this recipe are my choice. The beauty of Salade Russe is that you can really use whatever leftover cooked vegetables you have around. So please feel free to make substitutions. The important thing is not to have a preponderance of any one vegetable, and also not to use anything that becomes shredded or unrecognizable when cut into small pieces.

¼ cup each: cooked peas
cooked diced carrots
cooked corn kernels
chopped cooked string beans
cooked lima beans
diced cooked beets
chopped fresh tomato, seeded
chopped fresh onion

1 tsp. salt
3 tbsp. mayonnaise

1. Toss all the vegetables together to mix thoroughly. It is particularly important not to have any strong concentration of onions in one place.
2. Add the mayonnaise and toss some more, making sure the mayonnaise is mixed in well. Sprinkle with salt.
3. Refrigerate until time to serve.
4. The salad may be unmolded from the bowl and will keep its shape if the bowl is fairly shallow.

Vanilla-Rum Custard

1 cup milk
¼ cup sugar
2 eggs
½ tsp. vanilla
1 tbsp. dark rum

1. Put all the ingredients in a blender jar, and blend for 30 seconds.
2. Transfer mixture into individual custard cups (two large ones).
3. Preheat oven to 325 degrees.
4. Put about 1 inch of hot water into a baking pan. Set the filled custard cups in the water and carefilly put the pan into the oven. Bake 40 minutes.
5. Remove the custard cups from the water and place on a rack to cool. The custard may be served at room temperature in the cups, or (better) chilled in the refrigerator, unmolded, and served on individual dessert plates.

§ WARNING: Do not put the very hot custard cups directly into the refrigerator from the oven. First allow them to cool to room temperature.

~~ᦞ~~

DINNER XVIII

Individual Molds of Salmon Mousse
Roast Cornish Hens with Wild Rice Stuffing
Soufflé Potatoes
Hot Asparagus Tips with Crumbled Bacon
Lemon Soufflé
Coffee

~~ᦞ~~

Individual Molds of Salmon Mousse

For this recipe you will need two 1-cup molds of some decorative kind, or large custard cups may be used.

2 tbsp. minced onions
1 tbsp. butter
1 cup clam juice
1 envelope unflavored gelatin
4 tbsp. white wine
1 cup cooked salmon (boned), or canned salmon
½ tsp. salt
¼ tsp. white pepper
¼ cup mayonnaise

1. Sauté the onions in the butter until they are transparent, but not brown.
2. Soften the gelatin in the wine until all the grains are wet and soft. Add the gelatin to the pan with the onions and then add the clam juice. Bring to a simmer.
3. Transfer the liquid to a blender jar, add all the remaining ingredients except the mayonnaise and blend

for about a minute, until everything is well mixed and the mixture is smooth.

4. Pour mixture into the molds and refrigerate.

5. When set, unmold the mousse onto individual plates, garnish with mayonnaise, and perhaps a wedge of lemon, and serve.

Roast Cornish Hens with Wild Rice Stuffing

Cornish hens are usually available frozen, so please allow enough time for thawing them completely before cooking. The hens weigh about 1 pound or less, and one makes the ideal portion for one person.

STUFFING

> *2 tbsp. chopped shallots*
> *½ tsp. salt*
> *1 cup chicken broth*
> *2 tbsp. butter*
> *½ cup wild rice*

1. Preheat oven to 350 degrees.

2. In a saucepan, melt the butter and simmer the chopped shallots in it until they soften. Then add the chicken broth, salt, and wild rice. Stir well, cover, and simmer over low heat for about 15 minutes until the rice has absorbed the liquid. When ready, remove from heat and set aside.

HENS

2 *Cornish hens*
2 *tbsp. butter*
½ *tsp. salt*
¼ *tsp. poultry seasoning*
¼ *tsp. pepper*
1 *cup chicken broth*
2 *strips bacon, cut in half*

1. Dry the inside of the hens with a paper towel and season the cavities with salt and pepper. When the stuffing is ready, stuff the hens, and truss them.
2. Butter the outside of the hens and sprinkle with poultry seasoning. Place the strips of bacon over the breasts of the hens and place them on a rack in a roasting pan.
3. Roast for 45 minutes. During the roasting, baste frequently with drippings, adding some of the chicken broth if needed.
4. When the hens are done, remove them from the roasting pan. Add the chicken broth to the pan, place on burner, and bring to a boil. Quickly scrape all the drippings into the boiling broth to make the gravy.
5. To serve, partially cut the legs and thighs away from the bodies of the hens and break through the wing joints. Serve immediately with the hot gravy.

Soufflé Potatoes

2 *medium-sized potatoes, (oblong baking potatoes are ideal)*
2 *qts. cooking oil*
salt

1. Peel the potatoes and cut them into slices ⅛ inch thick.
2. Prepare two deep fryers, 1 qt. oil in each.

3. Put the sliced potatoes in one fryer of heated oil, increasing the heat until the potatoes rise to the top and float.

4. Meanwhile have the heat on high under the other fryer.

5. As soon as the potatoes float in the first fryer, take them out, drain them, and then quickly immerse them in the second fryer. The potatoes will puff up and turn golden brown.

6. When ready, remove from oil, drain a paper towel, and serve sprinkled with salt.

Hot Asparagus Tips with Crumbled Bacon

The best way to cook asparagus is to steam it in a special steamer which is tall and rather small in circumference, and contains a sectioned insert. This allows you to stand the asparagus spears up, with the thick bases in about 2 to 3 inches of water, and the tips at the top, never immersed in water. These steamers are relatively inexpensive and are good for cooking many other vegetables, such as corn on the cob, broccoli, zucchini, carrots, etc. I strongly recommend owning one. If you don't have one, then use a very deep pot and leave the bunch of asparagus tied together with a string so that you can stand the whole bunch up on the thick ends and untie it only after cooking.

4 strips lean bacon
1 bunch fresh asparagus (12 to 16 pieces)
2 tbsp. butter

1. Steam the asparagus for about 15 minutes in about 3 inches of water.

164

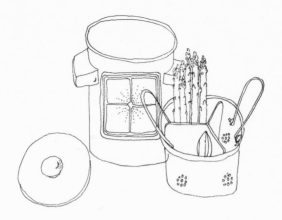

2. While the asparagus is steaming, fry the bacon until it is crisp, then drain it on paper towels and crumble it into a small bowl.

3. When the steaming is done, remove the asparagus from the pot and cut off about 4 inches from the thick ends.

4. Divide the asparagus into two portions. Put half the butter on the tips on each plate, and sprinkle with half the crumbled bacon. Serve hot.

Lemon Soufflé

This dessert is served cold and requires no baking. The whole trick is to fold the whipped cream and the egg whites into the lemon base carefully to avoid mashing out the air bubbles which provide the lightness.

1 envelope unflavored gelatin
grated rind of one lemon
½ cup lemon juice (this will require more than the
lemon you grated)
4 eggs, separated
½ tsp. salt
1 cup sugar
1 cup (½ pt.) heavy cream

1. You will need a deep soufflé dish, and it might be necessary to tie a paper collar around the top of the dish to extend the height. Be prepared to do this by cutting a piece of stiff brown paper a little longer than the circumference of the dish and having a piece of string or adhesive tape ready.

2. Soften the gelatin in about 4 tablespoons of cold water and make sure all the grains are soaked.

3. Over boiling water in a double boiler, beat together the egg yolks, lemon juice, half the sugar, and the salt. Continue to beat until the mixture thickens slightly, then stir in the softened gelatin and the grated lemon rind. Transfer to a large mixing bowl and allow to cool.

4. Beat the egg whites until they form soft peaks, then add the rest of the sugar and beat until stiff.

5. In a separate bowl, beat the heavy cream until thoroughly whipped and stiff.

6. Fold both the egg whites and the whipped cream into the lemon base. Do this gently, without stirring hard. The best implement for this job is a rubber scraper.

7. Now you can estimate visually whether you need the additional height of a paper collar on your soufflé dish to hold the dessert. If so, tie or tape the paper on, then pour in the soufflé. Refrigerate until ready to serve, preferably several hours to allow the gelatin to firm up.

DINNER XIX

Coquilles St. Jacques
Thin Veal Scallops with Lemon Butter
Fresh Steamed Spinach
Risotto Milanese
Endive Salad
Pear Tart
Coffee
White Wine

Coquilles St. Jacques

This recipe requires what the French call *crème fraîche*. This is an extra thick, heavy cream which is not normally available in the United States. However, it is very easy to make as follows: using a proportion of 1 teaspoon of buttermilk per cup of heavy cream, heat the combination of the two to lukewarm in a saucepan. Then let it stand at room temperature for 24 hours or until it thickens substantially. (Room temperature is defined as between 60 and 85 degrees Fahrenheit.) Note: If you do this in hot summer weather the cream could be ready in as little as 8 hours. Refrigerate until use.

18 to 20 fresh bay scallops
1 tbsp. finely chopped shallots (or onions if you must)
¼ tsp. saffron
½ cup white wine
1 tbsp. lemon juice
½ tsp. salt
¼ tsp. white pepper
1 tbsp. butter
2 tbsp. crème fraîche (see p. 167)
3 tbsp. grated Parmesan cheese

1. Simmer the scallops in a covered saucepan for 12 minutes with the shallots, saffron, wine, lemon juice, salt, and pepper.
2. Remove the scallops from the pan with a slotted spoon and transfer them to a Pyrex baking dish.
3. Simmer the remaining liquid in the pan several minutes more until the volume is reduced by one third.
4. Stir into the liquid the flour and butter, then the crème fraîche, and simmer (but do not boil) for 5 minutes.
5. Pour the sauce over the scallops in the baking dish, sprinkle the top with the Parmesan cheese, and put under a high broiler for 2 or 3 minutes until browned. Serve very hot.

§ NOTE: If you want to use individual ramekins or shells to serve this dish, in step 2 simply divide the scallops between two ramekins, and follow the remaining directions. Remember that the ramekins will be very hot and should be placed on another plate before bringing to the table.

Thin Veal Scallops with Lemon Butter

4 scallops veal, sliced no more than ¼ inch thick
4 tbsp. butter
4 tbsp. flour
grated rind of 1 lemon
1 tbsp. lemon juice

1. Soften 2 tablespoons of the butter at room temperature.
2. When soft, stir in half the grated lemon rind, mix well, and refrigerate.
3. Pound the veal scallops with the flat side of a heavy meat cleaver or with a meat hammer. Dust the meat on both sides with the flour.
4. Melt the remaining butter in a skillet, and sauté the veal in the butter. When the meat starts cooking, add the remaining lemon rind and the lemon juice to the pan.
5. Cook on each side for about 3 minutes. Transfer to warm serving plates, pour pan juices over the veal, top each slice with 1 teaspoon of the chilled lemon butter and serve hot.

Fresh Steamed Spinach

1 lb. fresh spinach
2 cloves garlic, peeled and cut in quarters
1 tbsp. vinegar
1 tbsp. olive oil

1. Wash the spinach leaves thoroughly in cold water. Cut off any thick stalks.
2. Steam the spinach on a steaming platform over boiling water for 15 minutes.
3. When the steaming is almost finished, heat the olive oil in a skillet and add the garlic pieces to the oil.
4. Remove the spinach from the steamer with a pair of tongs, shake off as much water as possible, and place in the skillet with the oil and garlic.
5. Toss the spinach in the hot oil and garlic (the tongs are ideal for this operation, too) for about 5 minutes, not allowing it to burn. Sprinkle with the vinegar, transfer to a warm serving dish, and serve.

Risotto Milanese
(Saffron Rice with Cheese)

Follow the directions for Risotto Milanese in Dinner VII, page 112.

Endive Salad

2 tbsp. olive oil
1 tbsp. vinegar
2 tsp. Maggi seasoning
½ tsp. salt
½ tsp. pepper
4 small heads endive
½ medium-sized onion, peeled and very thinly sliced
6 pitted green olives, thinly sliced

1. In a salad bowl mix the oil, vinegar, Maggi, salt, and pepper thoroughly.
2. Cut off the bases of the endive heads, separate the leaves and wash and drain them.

3. Add the leaves, torn in half, to the bowl, as well as the sliced onion and olives.

4. Toss well and serve.

Pear Tart

Follow the directions for the Raspberry Tart in Lunch III, page 48, substituting eight fresh or canned pear halves for the raspberries. If you use fresh pears, they must be carefully peeled and cored.

~~ᘓᕽᘗ~~

DINNER XX

Cuban Black Bean Soup
Rack of Barbecued Spare Ribs
Fresh Creamed Corn
Garlic Bread
Avocado-Mango Salad
Three-Flavor Ice Cream Parfait
Coffee

~~ᘓᕽᘗ~~

Cuban Black Bean Soup

½ cup dried black beans
2 tbsp. butter
¼ cup chopped celery
¾ cup chopped onions
1 tbsp. chopped parsley
1 2- or 3-inch piece ham bone
1 bay leaf
½ tsp. salt
¼ tsp. black pepper
1 tbsp. vinegar
¼ cup dry white wine (dry vermouth will do)

1. Wash the beans, then put them in a pot covered with cold water and let them stand overnight.
2. Drain off remaining water, then add 2 cups of fresh cold water and simmer over medium heat for 1 hour.
3. In a heavy saucepan, melt the butter and sauté the onions and celery in the butter for a few minutes until the onions become transparent but not browned.
4. Stir in the beans and their liquid, the parsley, add

the ham bone, bay leaf, salt, and pepper. Simmer this mixture, covered, for about 2 hours.

5. To serve, remove the ham bone, stir in the vinegar and the wine, bring to a simmer again, and serve.

Rack of Barbecued Spare Ribs

1 whole rack lean spare ribs
1 qt. barbecue sauce
  You can use ready-made barbecue sauce which is available in bottles at the supermarket. This sauce will do the job, but you can also make your own. To make your own, combine the following ingredients:
2 cups tomato paste
4 tbsp. vinegar
1 tsp. salt
2 tbsp. chopped onions
1 tsp. minced garlic
½ cup olive oil
½ tsp. pepper
1 tsp. chopped parsley
2 tbsp. brown sugar

1. Turn on the broiler of your stove to low and allow the broiling compartment to heat through completely.

2. If you are making your own barbecue sauce, mix all the ingredients in a saucepan and simmer over medium heat for 10 minutes, stirring well. If not, heat your bottled barbecue sauce the same way.

3. Wash and dry the rack of spare ribs and brush sauce onto both sides.

4. Place the meat on a rack in a roasting pan under the broiler. Keep meat as far away from the flame as your

equipment allows. Broil first on one side, until sauce begins to dry up and sizzle. Then baste with more sauce and turn over. Repeat this process until all but a small amount of the sauce is used up and the ribs have cooked through. You can test by cutting between two of the ribs with a sharp knife and checking for doneness.

5. Transfer the rack of ribs to a serving platter and cut the ribs apart with a knife before serving. Spoon the remaining sauce over the ribs.

Fresh Creamed Corn

4 ears corn on the cob
¼ cup heavy cream
2 tbsp. butter
½ tsp. salt
¼ tsp. pepper
1 tsp. chopped parsley
2 dashes Worcestershire sauce

1. Strip the ears of corn and drop them into 4 quarts of rapidly boiling water containing a little salt. Boil for ten minutes and remove from the pot.

2. Allow the corn to cool somewhat before handling. Then, with a sharp knife, cutting away from you, cut the kernels off the cob and put them in a small saucepan. Add the remaining ingredients and simmer.

3. Stir well and keep hot until ready to serve.

Garlic Bread

1 short loaf "baguette" French bread (or half a long one)
1 clove garlic
4 tbsp. butter
½ tsp. Lawry's Seasoned Salt

1. Melt the butter in a small saucepan, then pass the peeled clove of garlic through a garlic press and add it to the butter.
2. Split the bread in half lengthwise.
3. Carefully pour the garlic butter over the cut surfaces of the bread, then sprinkle them lightly with the seasoned salt.
4. Toast, cut side up, under a high broiler until just beginning to brown. Remove from broiler, cut in 2-inch slices, and serve in bread basket covered with a napkin to keep hot.

Avocado-Mango Salad

1 large firm but ripe avocado
1 medium-sized ripe mango
1 tbsp. olive oil
1 tsp. vinegar
1 tsp. lemon juice
½ tsp. salt
¼ tsp. white pepper
2 thin slices red pimiento
2 large leaves lettuce

1. Pit, peel, and slice the avocado and the mango.
2. Wash and pat dry the lettuce leaves, and place them each on an individual salad plate.
3. Arrange half the slices of mango and avocado, alternating, on each leaf.
4. Lay a slice of pimiento across the top of each salad.
5. Mix the remaining ingredients in a small bowl, and pour half over each salad.

Three-Flavor Ice Cream Parfait

The trick here is in the appearance, which makes this dessert festive and more than "just ice cream." Use your three favorite flavors, one of them sherbet if you like, and try to pick some brightly contrasting colors. That is, if your favorites are butter-pecan, vanilla, and banana, make a sacrifice for the sake of color! Next, it is important to have stemmed, clear glass parfait glasses—the tall narrow kind. Now, in your freezer, set up some way to be able to put your parfait glasses in at an angle without danger of moving once they are set in.

3 ½-pt. containers of three flavors of ice cream
½ cup heavy cream, whipped
2 maraschino cherries

1. Soften the ice cream by leaving out containers for a couple of hours.
2. Pour flavor number 1 into the parfait glasses about ⅓ full. Now place the glasses in the freezer lying tilted at an angle, so that the contents do not spill, and reach about halfway up the side of the glass. Allow to freeze until the ice cream stays at the same angle even when glass is placed upright.
3. Now insert flavor number 2 in a similar way and freeze.

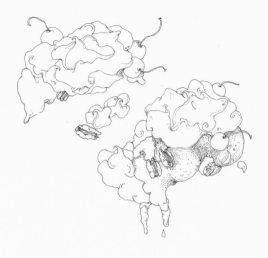

4. For the last flavor, fill the parfait glass to the top and put it in the freezer upright.

5. Have the whipped cream ready in the refrigerator during dinner so that it can be added at the last moment.

6. Just before serving, put half the whipped cream on top of each parfait and top with a cherry.

DINNER XXI

Eggs à la Russe
Grilled Veal Chops
Puréed Potatoes with Sour Cream and
Minced Onion
Steamed Broccoli Hollandaise
Bananes Flambées
Coffee

Eggs à la Russe

4 hard-cooked eggs
2 large lettuce leaves
4 tbsp. mayonnaise
1 tbsp. chili sauce
2 tsp. chopped parsley
½ tsp. salt
¼ tsp. white pepper
1 tsp. lemon juice

1. Peel and put the hard-cooked eggs through an egg slicer to make round slices.
2. Wash lettuce and arrange 2 sliced eggs on each leaf on small plates.
3. Mix remaining ingredients together thoroughly. Spoon sauce evenly over egg slices and serve.

Grilled Veal Chops

2 large veal chops (or 4 if they are small)
1 tbsp. olive oil
½ tsp. white pepper

1. Rub both sides of the chops with olive oil (to prevent sticking to the grill) while you have the grill on the stove heating over a high heat. I recommend using a stove-top grill, cast iron or aluminum, with raised ridges and a runoff channel.
2. Then rub both sides of the meat with the white pepper.
3. Place the chops on the grill and cook about 10 minutes on each side, depending on thickness. You do not want veal to be rare, but it should not be cooked through as much as pork.
4. Serve as soon as possible after cooking.

Puréed Potatoes with Sour Cream and Minced Onion

4 medium-sized potatoes, peeled
4 tbsp. finely chopped onions
2 tbsp. butter
¾ cup sour cream
½ tsp. salt
½ tsp. pepper

1. Boil the potatoes in rapidly boiling slightly salted water until tender.
2. When ready, drain off water quickly, leaving potatoes in the pan.
3. Add the butter, sour cream, salt, and pepper and mash to a smooth purée with a potato masher.
4. Finally, stir in the chopped onions and keep over very low heat for about 3 minutes to slightly cook the onions.
5. Keep warm until ready to serve.

Steamed Broccoli Hollandaise

HOLLANDAISE SAUCE

Follow the directions for hollandaise sauce in the Fillet of Sole recipe in Lunch III, page 45 .

BROCCOLI

6 medium stalks broccoli, washed

Steam the broccoli over boiling water on a steaming platform or in a vertical steamer for 15 minutes. Remove from heat and serve hot, with the hollandaise sauce.

Bananes Flambées

2 firm but ripe bananas, peeled and split
2 tbsp. butter
1 tbsp. lemon juice
2 tbsp. brown sugar
¼ cup brandy, warmed

1. In a skillet, melt the butter, then add the lemon juice and sugar and cook for 2 minutes.
2. Now add the 4 pieces of banana, and sauté for 5 minutes, flat side down, basting occasionally with the liquids in the pan.
3. To serve, bring to the table, pour the warm brandy over and ignite it. When the flames subside, serve on dessert plates.

~◦e~

DINNER XXII
Écrevisses (or Shrimp) à la Nage
Roast Saddle of Lamb for Two
Baked Potatoes
Watercress and Endive Salad
Vanilla Soufflé
Vintage Red Wine
Coffee

~◦e~

Écrevisses à la Nage (Crayfish in Broth)

Crayfish, contrary to some opinions, are among the tastiest crustaceans in existence. They look like very small lobsters. Their tails range from 1 to 1½ inches in length. They can be found in warm climates with sluggish rivers such as Louisiana, Florida, Texas, and parts of Southern California. With a great deal of diligence and patience, they can also be found fresh-frozen. The crayfish inhabit fresh water, and the tails are sweet and tender. Once you have tasted them, you will be an avid seeker of further supplies. This recipe can be made with equivalent amounts of shrimps, but try to get the whole shrimps, including the heads.

20 *crayfish, live or frozen*
4 *tbsp. butter*
2 *cups dry white wine*
1 *carrot, peeled and thinly sliced*
1 *cup chopped onions*
1 *tbsp. chopped parsley*
1 *tbsp. chopped fresh dill*
1 *bay leaf*
½ *tsp. salt*
½ *tsp. pepper*

1. Bring about 3 quarts of water to a boil in a saucepan. Drop the crayfish into it and boil for 3 minutes. Remove the crayfish and discard the water. Allow the crayfish to cool a few minutes to avoid burning your fingers when you handle them. Then separate the tails from the bodies with a quick twist. Carefully peel the shells away from the tails, and remove the intestinal veins down the backs, saving the little strip of meat that covers the vein. Put all the cleaned tails and extra strips of meat into a bowl and set aside.

2. Take all the shells and place them in a shallow baking pan. Then dry them in a 350-degree oven for about 45 minutes. When they are dry, run them through the medium blade of your meat grinder, or use a blender to grind them. Be careful not to lose a finger in the process. Last choice is to put them in a large mortar and crush them with a pestle.

3. Melt the butter in a large cast iron skillet, add the ground shells and 1 cup of water and simmer for about 20 minutes. Then strain the liquid into a saucepan and discard the ground shells.

4. Add the wine and all the remaining ingredients to the saucepan, including the cooked tails.

5. Bring to a simmer, cook for 5 minutes, and serve immediately as a soup.

§ OPTIONAL: If you want to make the soup richer, beat together about ½ cup of crème fraîche and an egg yolk and add it to the soup before simmering.

Roast Saddle of Lamb for Two

A whole saddle of lamb would easily serve 4 to 6 people, so the only problem is to get your butcher to sell you half a saddle of lamb. The saddle is the loin chop area, with the chops not cut apart. Trim the fat down to a thin layer, and tie the saddle to make ready for the oven.

½ saddle lamb
1 tsp. pepper
1 tbsp. rosemary
½ cup white wine
2 tbsp. butter

1. Preheat oven to 450 degrees. Sprinkle the meat with the rosemary and the pepper.

2. Roast the saddle on a rack in the roasting pan for 55 minutes, lowering the temperature to 400 degrees. for the last 15 minutes of the period.

3. When ready, remove saddle from the pan and keep warm on a serving platter while preparing the sauce.

4. Add the wine and the butter to the pan juices and simmer over medium heat until volume is reduced by half. Transfer to gravy boat and serve with the roast.

5. When serving roast, simply carve the saddle into

separate the chops. The servings will have the appearance of small loin chops.

Baked Potatoes

2 large well-shaped baking potatoes
1 tbsp. olive oil
2 tbsp. butter
½ tsp. salt

1. Scrub the potatoes thoroughly under cold water, then dry.
2. Preheat oven to 450 degrees. (Note: This is the same temperature you are using for the roast saddle of lamb. Your oven should be large enough to accommodate the potatoes as well.)
3. Rub both potatoes briskly with olive oil, punch holes in the tops with a fork, and place in middle level of preheated oven.
4. Bake for 1 hour, or until a knife plunged into the potato goes in easily without meeting any resistance near the center. When ready, slit the top, break open, insert 1 tablespoon butter in each potato, sprinkle with salt, and serve.

Watercress and Endive Salad

1 bunch watercress
2 heads endive
2 tbsp. olive oil
1 tbsp. vinegar
½ tsp. salt
¼ tsp. pepper
1 tsp. lemon juice
1 tsp. chopped chives
1 tsp. Maggi seasoning

1. Wash the watercress in cold running water, then trim off stems, leaving the leaves and the thinnest portion of the stems.

2. Cut off the bottoms of the heads of endive, then separate the leaves from each other. Wash under cold water and drain, together with the watercress, in a colander.

3. In a salad bowl, mix all the remaining ingredients until thoroughly blended. Then add the salad, toss, and serve.

Vanilla Soufflé

For this recipe you will need a 3-cup soufflé dish.

2 tbsp. softened butter
6 tbsp. granulated sugar
2 tbsp. flour
½ cup milk
3 eggs, separated
1 tbsp. vanilla extract
2 tbsp. powdered (confectioners') sugar

1. Butter the inside of the soufflé dish, sprinkle in 1 tablespoon powdered sugar and swish it around all inside surfaces. Knock out excess sugar which doesn't adhere.

2. Preheat oven to 400 degrees.

3. Using a saucepan, mix the flour with a little milk and stir into a paste. Add the rest of the milk and 4 tablespoons sugar, then bring the mixture to a boil, still stirring. When boil is reached, remove from heat.

4. With saucepan away from the heat, beat the egg yolks into the milk mixture, then stir in the other tablespoon butter.

5. Separately, beat the egg whites until they form soft peaks, then add the other tablespoon sugar and beat until stiff.

6. Stir the vanilla extract into the milk mixture, then fold the egg whites into it. Pour the assembled batter into the soufflé dish and bake about 20 minutes until it rises 2 or 3 inches above the edge of the dish. Serve *immediately*.

~~~

DINNER XXIII

Hot Russian Borscht
Chicken à la Kiev
Potato Pancakes
String Bean Salad
Fresh Strawberries with Sour Cream and
Brown Sugar
Tea

~~~

Hot Russian Borscht

2 cans beef consommé (or your own beef stock if you have time)
1 cup uncooked cubed beets (washed and scraped before cubing)
1 tsp. Maggi seasoning
4 European dried mushrooms
½ cup shredded cabbage
½ tsp. black pepper

1. Assemble all the ingredients in a deep saucepan, bring to a simmer and cook covered for about 2 hours over

low heat. If necessary you may add a little water or consommé.

2. Before serving, remove the mushrooms, which are now softened by the cooking, chop finely and return them to the soup.

3. The soup is ready to serve and is delicious with the addition of a large spoonful of sour cream to each plate.

§ OTHER OPTIONAL ADDITIONS: Any cooked beef or pork leftovers available; or small pieces of Polish sausage or chopped hard-cooked egg may be added.

Chicken à la Kiev

This dish is very simple, but contains an element of surprise which is guaranteed to delight your guest, especially if he (or she) has never encountered it before. You may prepare it the day of the dinner, or it can be prepared, frozen, and cooked very quickly after removal from the freezer. The essential point to remember is to fully seal the butter inside the envelope of chicken so that it does not escape during the cooking. The portions given here allow one medium to small chicken breast per person.

2 boned chicken breasts (have your butcher do it)
1 tsp. Lawry's Seasoned Salt
½ tsp. white pepper
¼ lb. butter
4 tbsp. flour
2 beaten eggs
oil for deep frying
1 cup matzoh meal (or fine white breadcrumbs)

1. Cut the chicken breasts in half if the butcher hasn't done it. Take 1 piece at a time, put it between 2 pieces

of waxed paper and pound it with the flat side of a heavy meat cleaver or the bottom of a heavy frying pan until it is quite thin. Be very careful not to tear the chicken.

2. Cut the butter into 4 2-tablespoon-sized pieces. (A ¼-lb. stick of butter contains 8 tablespoons which are frequently marked off on the wrapping paper. To be accurate, I suggest cutting the butter with a sharp knife right through the paper on the lines, and removing the paper afterwards.) Put the 4 pieces of butter into your freezer and let them harden.

3. Now sprinkle one side of each piece of chicken with salt and pepper. Then, seasoned side in, wrap one piece of butter in each piece of chicken, tucking the ends in carefully to prevent leakage.

4. In your deep fryer, heat the oil to 375 degrees, using a fat thermometer for accuracy. The fat should be deep enough to cover the rolled chicken by an inch. Roll each piece of chicken in the flour, then dip it in the beaten eggs, and then roll it in the matzoh meal. Then put the pieces in the refrigerator (or freezer) and chill thoroughly. At this point, you can simply freeze them for later use.

5. To prepare, deep fry the chicken until it turns golden brown, remove from oil, drain on paper towels, and serve hot. Be very careful when removing the chicken from the oil. It is best to lift out the frying basket completely and then tip it gently to allow the pieces to roll out onto the paper towels.

§ NOTE: At the table, be sure to warn your guest that he shouldn't cut into the chicken too hard the first time, or he will be rewarded with a spurt of hot melted butter which might wind up redesigning his tie! It is better to slit it with a sharp knife first and let the butter run out.

Potato Pancakes

2 *medium-sized potatoes*
½ *medium-sized onion*
½ *tsp. salt*
1 *egg*
2 *tbsp. butter*

1. Peel and wash the potatoes.
2. Grate the raw potatoes and the half onion through the finest blade of your grater. Beat the egg and the salt into the mixture.
3. Heat the butter in a skillet, lower heat to medium, and cook the pancakes, one large cooking-spoon full at a time. When the edges are beginning to brown on the first side, flip and cook the other.
4. Place the finished pancakes in a Pyrex dish kept warm in the oven until all are done. Serve hot.

String Bean Salad

1 *lb. fresh string beans*
2 *tbsp. fresh chopped dill*
¼ *tsp. salt*
¼ *tsp. pepper*
1 *tbsp. lemon juice*
2 *tbsp. olive oil*

1. Wash the beans and cut off the ends.
2. Steam the beans on a steaming platform over boiling water in a deep covered saucepan for no more than 8 minutes. They should be cooked, but crisp, and should *not* have turned to an olive color.

3. Refrigerate the beans to cool them but don't let them get ice-cold.

4. Mix the remaining ingredients thoroughly in a salad bowl, reserving half of the chopped dill. Add the string beans and toss well, then sprinkle the rest of the dill over the top, and serve.

Fresh Strawberries with Sour Cream and Brown Sugar

1 pt. fresh strawberries
½ cup brown sugar
1 cup sour cream

1. Wash and hull the strawberries, then slice them in half.

2. Place the strawberries in a bowl, sprinkle the brown sugar over them, and toss lightly to spread the sugar throughout. Leave refrigerated for a couple of hours or overnight.

3. To serve, transfer to individual bowls and top each with half the sour cream.

❦

DINNER XXIV
Beef Consommé with Barley
Grilled Striped Bass with Lemon Butter
Cappellini with Parmesan
Salade Niçoise
Bananas and Whipped Cream
White Wine
Coffee

❦

Beef Consommé with Barley

2 cups beef consommé (or homemade beef broth)
¼ cup peeled and thinly sliced carrots
2 dried European mushrooms
½ cup barley
½ tsp. salt
¼ tsp. pepper

1. Soak the barley in cold water overnight.
2. Pour about ½ cup of boiling water over the dried mushrooms in a bowl and soak them for 2 hours. Reserve the liquid.
3. Bring the consommé to a simmer in a saucepan over medium-low heat.
4. Add the carrots, salt, and pepper and simmer 5 minutes.
5. Remove the mushrooms from their liquid and chop them finely, then add them to the soup. Strain the mushroom liquid through a piece of cheesecloth and add it to the soup.

6. Drain the barley and add it to the soup.

7. Cover and simmer over low heat for 20 minutes, then serve hot.

Grilled Striped Bass with Lemon Butter

1 3- to 4-lb. fresh striped bass, cleaned
½ cup finely chopped onions
2 strips hickory-smoked bacon
2 tbsp. olive oil
½ tsp. salt
½ tsp. pepper
4 tbsp. butter
1 tbsp. grated lemon rind

1. Wash the fish, including the belly cavity, under cold running water.

2. Lay the two bacon strips in the cavity, then pack in the chopped onions.

3. Using 3 or 4 short pieces of string, tie the fish to keep the onions and bacon from falling out.

4. Brush the surface of the fish with olive oil to prevent sticking to the grill.

5. Soften the butter at room temperature, blend into it the grated lemon rind, pack into small earthenware crock or cup, and refrigerate until fish is served.

6. To cook the fish you need a stove-top grill. Heat the grill over high heat.

7. Grill fish on each side for about 6 or 7 minutes, depending on size. Test for doneness by carefully flaking one place with a fork. Make sure fish has cooked all the way through to the bone. When ready, the fish should have a crisp outer skin and the meat should be tender and juicy. Snip off strings and bring the whole fish

to the table on a warm platter. Serve with the lemon butter.

Cappellini with Parmesan

A word about cappellini. Italian spaghetti is available in many different sizes. Cappellini is one of the thinnest. You must buy it from a store which carries a full selection. Do not expect to find it on the shelves of your local supermarket. If you live in a city which has an Italian district, you are in luck. Generally, cappellini is indicated by a "No. 11" on the box. The meaning of the name in English is "angels' hair," so how can you go wrong?

½ lb. cappellini
4 tbsp. butter
¾ cup freshly grated Parmesan cheese
½ cup heavy cream
1 tsp. freshly grated black pepper
1 tsp. salt
1 tbsp. olive oil

1. In a large pot boil about 3 quarts of water, and add the olive oil and the salt to it.
2. Drop in the cappellini and let it boil at high heat for exactly 8 minutes. Then pour the contents of the pot out into a colander previously prepared and waiting in the sink. Quickly run some hot water over the cooked cappellini in the colander and then let it drain about a minute.
3. Transfer the cappellini to a large enameled skillet. Add the butter, the cream, the pepper, and the grated Parmesan.

4. Bring to a low simmer and stir gently to blend all ingredients, then serve hot.

Salade Niçoise

1 cup cooked French-cut string beans
½ cup cooked diced potatoes
6 anchovy fillets
1 tomato, sliced
1 hard-cooked egg, chopped
½ cup canned tuna chunks
12 pitted ripe green olives
2 tbsp. olive oil
1 tbsp. vinegar
½ tsp. salt
¼ tsp. pepper

1. In a salad bowl, mix the oil, vinegar, salt, and pepper.
2. Cut the string beans into 1-inch lengths and add, with the potatoes, anchovies, tomato, egg, tuna, and olives to the bowl.
3. Toss thoroughly and serve.

Bananas and Whipped Cream

½ pt. heavy cream
2 fresh bananas, firm and not overripe
½ cup brown sugar
4 tbsp. butter
4 tbsp. Grand Marnier

1. Whip the cream with an electric or hand-held beater and refrigerate until time to serve dessert.
2. Peel the bananas and split them in half lengthwise.
3. Melt the butter in an enameled skillet, then add the

sugar and the Grand Marnier, and finally the bananas. Cook them for about 5 minutes, then transfer to serving platter and serve hot with chilled whipped cream.

~ꬹ~

DINNER XXV

Oysters on the Half Shell
Chicken Broth with Dumplings
Boiled Brisket of Beef with
Horseradish Sauce
Boiled Potatoes and Carrots
Orange-Almond Cake
Coffee

~ꬹ~

Oysters on the Half Shell

1 doz. fresh oysters
½ cup chili sauce
1 tsp. grated horseradish
1 lemon, quartered into wedges

1. Arrange two oyster dishes with crushed ice, or use two soup plates filled with crushed ice but with space hollowed out in the middle for a cup of sauce.
2. Open the oysters, discard the top shell, and quickly wash with the coldest possible water. Do not cut the meat away from the bottom shell.
3. Mix the chili sauce and horseradish, and divide into 2 small cups, placed in the middle of the crushed ice.
4. Arrange 6 oysters on each plate surrounding the cup of sauce, garnish with lemon wedges, and serve. Make

sure you have oyster forks, the type with a cutting edge on one side to remove the oysters from the shells.

Chicken Broth with Dumplings

For this recipe you may use a good-quality canned chicken broth which now is available. If you hate cans, then make your own broth by simmering a whole stewing chicken for several hours in water with some carrots, celery, parsley, salt, and pepper and a bay leaf, then straining.

> 2 cups chicken broth
> 1 tbsp. butter
> 1 egg, separated
> 1 tbsp. flour

1. Vigorously mix the egg yolk and the butter with a fork until smooth.
2. Now beat the egg white until fluffy, then carefully stir the flour into it, trying not to crush the egg whites.
3. Now gently fold the whites into the yolks.
4. Bring the broth to a simmer, then drop the dumplings into it, 1 teaspoon of batter at a time, then cover the saucepan and let the broth simmer about 3 minutes. Serve hot.

Boiled Brisket of Beef with Horseradish Sauce

1 2-lb. piece first cut brisket, trimmed of fat
2 stalks celery
4 large carrots
1 large onion, quartered
1 bay leaf
3 cups canned beef broth
2 tbsp. olive oil
1 pt. heavy cream
¼ cup freshly grated horseradish

1. Heat the olive oil in a heavy skillet large enough to contain the entire piece of brisket. When it gets hot, brown the meat on all sides for a few minutes, using tongs, not a fork, to turn it.
2. Place the meat in a heavy enameled pot, peel the carrots and add them, the celery, and the onion. Add the bay leaf and the beef broth and bring to a simmer. Simmer covered over low heat for 3 hours.
3. When meat will be ready in 20 minutes, beat the heavy cream until it forms soft peaks, fold in the grated horseradish and keep sauce in refrigerator until the meat is served.
4. To serve brisket, remove from pot and slice across the grain into ¼-inch-thick slices. Add a spoonful of the broth to each portion and serve the horseradish sauce on the side.

Boiled Potatoes and Carrots

2 large (or 4 small) mature potatoes
1 tsp. salt

1. Peel and cut the large potatoes in half (leave small ones whole).
2. Boil in salted water until tender. Drain and serve with the brisket.
3. Also serve the carrots which were cooked with the meat.

Orange-Almond Cake

CAKE

    1½ cups ground, blanched, and peeled almonds
    ¾ cup sugar
    2 tbsp. lemon juice
    2 tbsp. softened butter

1. Preheat oven to 200 degrees.
2. Butter the inside of an 8-inch × 6-inch baking pan.
3. Mix all the remaining ingredients together thoroughly in a bowl, then spread over bottom and about 1 inch up the sides of the baking pan.
4. Bake in preheated oven for 30 minutes. Remove from oven and set aside to cool before filling.

FILLING

    2 oranges
    1½ cups sugar
    ½ cup water

1. Grate the whole oranges, rind and all, through medium-fine blade of your grater. Remove the pits.
2. Combine the grated orange with the sugar and the water and cook until a thick syrupy texture results (about 8 to 10 minutes), stirring frequently.

3. Remove from heat, allow to cool about 5 minutes, then pour into cooled almond crust and spread evenly over the surface. Refrigerate until ready to serve.

❧

DINNER XXVI

Purée of Pea Soup Garnished with
Sliced Garlic Sausage
Truite au Bleu
Boiled Potatoes
Grilled Tomatoes
Chocolate Parfait
White Wine
Coffee

❧

Purée of Pea Soup Garnished with Sliced Garlic Sausage

2 cups chicken broth
2 lbs. freshly shelled peas
1 tsp. salt
4 tbsp. butter
1 chorizo (Spanish garlic sausage) about 8 inches long, or similar sausage

1. Simmer the washed peas in the chicken broth with the salt and the butter over low heat for about an hour until the peas are very soft. Do not boil.
2. Transfer contents of the pot into your blender jar (use two blendings if jar gets too full) and blend at high speed for about 1 minute.

3. Return blended soup to pot, and reheat over low heat. While heating, slice the chorizo into ¼-inch slices and add to the pot. Cook about 20 minutes, stirring occasionally, and serve hot. This soup may be kept hot for an hour or more before serving without damage, but it may require the addition of a little broth if it gets too thick.

Truite au Bleu

This recipe is a classic and happens to be perfect for two people. Because of the last-minute character of the preparations, it is difficult to make for more than two and still serve everyone at the same time. The most important consideration here is getting fresh, preferably live, trout. Trout will live in a container of fresh water after being caught. Take the trouble and you will be rewarded.

4 qts. water
1 cup vinegar
1 tbsp. salt
1 tsp. peppercorns
2 large peeled carrots
2 large peeled onions
1 bay leaf
1 sprig fresh parsley
2 live trout
2 lemon wedges
¼ lb. melted butter

1. Combine the first 8 ingredients in a large pot and boil.
2. Just a few minutes before serving, take the live trout

from the water tank and hit them on the head to stun them. Quickly clean them (do not remove heads or tails) by slitting open the bellies and pulling out the innards with one finger. Then rinse under cold water and drop them into the boiling liquid. Cook about 4 minutes.

3. Garnish with the lemon wedges and bathe in melted butter. Serve immediately.

Boiled Potatoes

The potatoes to accompany Truite au Bleu must be small and firm.

8 small young (but not "new") potatoes
½ tsp. salt

1. Peel the potatoes, removing any eyes, and, even though it is wasteful, peel them down so that they are all the same size.

2. Put them in a pan full of cold, salted water and boil until they are cooked through but still firm (about 20 minutes).

3. Drain and serve immediately with the trout. If there will be any delay, cover them with a napkin to keep in the heat until serving time.

Grilled Tomatoes

1 large or 2 medium-small tomatoes
1 tbsp. very finely chopped onion
1 tsp. very finely minced garlic
1 tsp. grated Parmesan cheese
¼ tsp. pepper
1 tbsp. softened butter

1. Cut the tomatoes in half. Light the broiler and set it on low.

2. Stir the softened butter, onions, garlic, pepper, and cheese until they become a loose paste.

3. Carefully spread the cut surfaces of the tomatoes as evenly as possible with this mixture.

4. Place the tomatoes, cut side up, in a baking dish or broiling pan.

5. Broil about 8 inches away from the heat for 8 minutes.

6. Remove from broiler and serve hot.

Chocolate Parfait

1 pt. best-quality chocolate ice cream
½ pt. heavy cream
1 tbsp. sugar
4 oz. dark cooking chocolate
4 tbsp. strong coffee
2 maraschino cherries

1. Whip the cream and the sugar together until fluffy and refrigerate.

2. In the top of a double boiler over simmering, not boiling, water melt the chocolate in the coffee and stir vigorously to get a smooth sauce. Allow to cool after melting.

3. To assemble parfaits, use two tall parfait glasses. Put about ½ to ¾ inch of the chocolate sauce in the bottom of each. Then fill within an inch of the top with ice cream. Fill with chocolate sauce, top with whipped cream forced through a pastry tube in a decorative pattern, and add a cherry.

4. Store the parfaits in the freezer until serving time.

〜〜◦〜〜

DINNER XXVII

Clams William
Beef en Brochette
Wild Rice
Black Radish and Baby Tomato Salad
Chocolate Bavarian Cream
Red Wine
Coffee

〜〜◦〜〜

Although this recipe gives the proper quantities for two, William (for whom it is named) has been known to consume four times the amount!

Clams William

2 doz. fresh littleneck clams on the half shell (top shells discarded)
¾ cup dry white wine
2 tbsp. fresh chopped chives
1 tbsp. chopped shallots
½ cup clam juice
2 tbsp. lemon juice
6 tbsp. butter
1 tsp. freshly ground white pepper
½ tsp. salt

1. Melt the butter in a large skillet (for which you have a cover). Do not allow the butter to brown.
2. Stir in all the remaining ingredients except the pepper and salt.

3. Place the clams on the half shell in the liquid, sprinkle with the seasonings, and bring to a gentle simmer.

4. Cover and cook for 10 minutes.

5. Serve in soup plates. Put a dozen clams in each plate, then spoon over the remaining liquid from the pan. Provide a soup spoon and a small fork for the clams.

Beef en Brochette

For this recipe you need two shashlik skewers about 10 inches long.

> 1 *lb. fillet of beef cut into 1-inch cubes*
> 6 *cherry tomatoes*
> 6 *baby onions*
> 6 *mushroom caps, about 1 inch in diameter*
> 2 *tbsp. butter*

1. Melt the butter in a small skillet which has a cover. Over very low heat, cook the mushrooms and the peeled baby onions, covered, for about 10 minutes until the onions are partially softened, but not falling apart. Look into the pan after about 5 minutes, baste, and turn the mushrooms and onions so that they cook evenly.

2. During the last 3 minutes of step 1, add the cherry tomatoes to the pan. When the time is up, remove from heat, uncover, and let stand.

3. Turn your broiler to high. Arrange the meat and vegetables on the skewers as follows: 1 meat cube, 1 onion, 1 mushroom cap, 1 tomato, 1 meat cube, and repeat in that order until all the meat and vegetables have been used and are evenly divided between the two skewers. Reserve the liquid remaining in the skillet.

4. Place the filled skewers in a shallow baking or broil-

ing pan. Brush the meat with the reserved liquid, then place under the broiler. For rare meat, cook about 3 minutes on each of the four sides, longer if you like it medium or well done.

5. To serve, it is customary to bring the skewers to the dining table on a platter, then grasp each by the ring on the end with a pot holder or napkin, and push the meat and vegetables off the skewer and onto the plate with a two-tined fork. Make sure the dinner plates have been warmed.

Wild Rice

½ cup wild rice
1 clove garlic, peeled and chopped
2 tbsp. butter
1 tsp. salt
4 dried European mushrooms

1. Bring 1 quart of water to a boil in a saucepan. Add the salt, butter, mushrooms, garlic, and rice.
2. Lower heat to medium and cook for 40 minutes until the rice is soft.
3. Just before serving, fish out the mushrooms, which

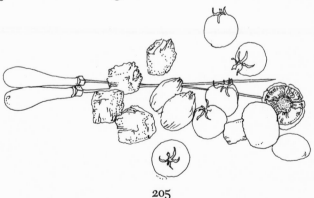

should now be quite soft, chop them very finely on a board, drain the remaining water from the rice, stir in the chopped mushrooms, add a little more butter and serve with the beef en brochette.

Black Radish and Baby Tomato Salad

1 box cherry tomatoes
2 medium-sized black radishes
½ cup sour cream
2 tsp. Maggi seasoning
½ tsp. Lawry's Seasoned Salt
¼ tsp. black pepper
2 tsp. lemon juice
¼ cup finely chopped scallions

1. In the salad bowl, mix the sour cream, Maggi, salt, pepper, lemon juice, and scallions.
2. Cut the cherry tomatoes in half and add to the dressing in the bowl.
3. Peel the black radishes with a potato peeler. Slice them into thin slices and add to the dressing.
4. Toss well and serve.

Chocolate Bavarian Cream

For this dessert you will need a 1-pt. mold.

1 envelope unflavored gelatin
3 tbsp. cold water
1 tsp. vanilla extract
½ cup milk
2 egg yolks
¼ cup sugar
1 oz. semisweet chocolate
¾ cup heavy cream

1. Soften the gelatin powder in the water and keep handy.

2. In a small saucepan, heat the milk and the vanilla extract just short of the boiling point, then reduce heat to very low and have ready to add to custard.

3. In the top of a double boiler, over simmering water, beat the egg yolks and sugar together. Then add the hot milk, a little at a time, and then the chocolate. Stir until the chocolate has melted and is well blended throughout.

4. Remove from heat, stir in the softened gelatin, and refrigerate.

5. In a mixing bowl, beat the heavy cream until it is quite stiff.

6. When the chocolate mixture has chilled, fold the whipped cream into it, and turn into lightly oiled 1-pt. mold. Refrigerate and allow it to set firmly, 4 to 6 hours.

7. To serve, unmold onto serving plate.

~೨ၑჀ~

DINNER XVIII

Fresh Shrimp Cocktail with
Lemon Mayonnaise
Grilled Bacon-Wrapped Fillets of Beef
Baked Potatoes with Sour Cream and Chives
Green Salad with Roquefort Dressing
Vanilla Peaches
Red Wine
Coffee

~Ⴠၑ೨~

Fresh Shrimp Cocktail with
Lemon Mayonnaise

1 doz. fresh jumbo shrimps
1 bay leaf
1 tsp. peppercorns
1 stalk fresh dill
½ cup mayonnaise
1 tsp. grated lemon rind
½ tsp. grated horseradish
½ tsp. lemon juice

1. Peel and clean the shrimps, carefully removing the intestinal tract from the back of the shrimps.
2. Boil 1 quart of water and drop in the bay leaf, peppercorns, and dill stalk. Then put in the cleaned shrimps and boil for 4 minutes.
3. Remove the shrimps from the water and refrigerate to chill.
4. Mix the remaining ingredients together in a bowl.

5. To serve, arrange the shrimps in cocktail glasses or on small dishes and top with lemon mayonnaise.

Grilled Bacon-Wrapped Fillets of Beef

1 tbsp. olive oil
2 1½ inch thick fillets of beef
2 strips hickory smoked bacon
black pepper

1. Heat your stove-top grill over medium heat until very hot. Brush the grill with olive oil.
2. Wrap one strip of bacon around the side of each fillet and secure with a wooden toothpick. (Plastic toothpicks melt!)
3. After rubbing both sides with pepper, grill the steaks about 4 minutes on each side. This will give you rare steaks. You will need additional cooking time for medium. Serve hot, with a little butter on top.

Baked Potatoes with Sour Cream and Chives

2 large baking potatoes
1 cup sour cream
2 tbsp. fresh chopped chives
1 tsp. Lawry's Seasoned Salt
1 tbsp. olive oil

1. Preheat oven to 450 degrees.
2. Scrub the potatoes under running cold water. Dry, then rub the skins with olive oil.
3. Place them on the rack in the preheated oven and bake for 1 hour. With a fork punch some holes in the tops of the potatoes to let steam escape.
4. When done, remove potatoes from oven and make

two cuts in the form of a cross in the tops with a sharp knife, then squeeze the sides to open up the potato.

5. Mix the sour cream, chives, and seasoned salt together and serve as dressing with the potatoes.

Green Salad with Roquefort Dressing

1 small head bibb lettuce
1 tbsp. chopped parsley
1 tbsp. minced scallions
1 small bunch watercress
2 tbsp. olive oil
1 tbsp. vinegar
½ tsp. salt
½ tsp. black pepper
2 oz. Roquefort cheese (make sure it's real Roquefort, don't accept substitutes!)

1. Wash the lettuce and the watercress and drain in a colander.

2. While the greens are draining, mix the oil, vinegar, salt, pepper, and Roquefort cheese in a salad bowl, breaking the cheese up with a fork and mixing until the cheese is well blended into the liquids.

3. Add the lettuce, watercress, scallions, and parsley to the salad bowl, toss well, and serve.

Vanilla Peaches

4 canned or stewed peach halves
2 scoops (½ pt.) vanilla ice cream
½ cup apricot preserves, forced through a sieve
1 tbsp. sugar

1. Place one scoop of the ice cream in each of two

dessert bowls, and flank with two peach halves, cut-side turned in. Store in the freezer for a few minutes while preparing the sauce.
2. Heat the apricot preserves and sugar together until almost boiling.
3. Pour the hot sauce over the peaches and ice cream and serve immediately.

DINNER XXIX

Melon Ball Cocktail
Grilled Fillets of Flounder with
Béarnaise Sauce
Buttered Parsley Potatoes
Steamed Cauliflower
Fresh Mushroom and Lettuce Salad
Sugared Strawberries and Cream
White Wine
Coffee

Melon Ball Cocktail

½ each of 3 kinds of melon: cantaloupe, honeydew, and
  Crenshaw
2 orange slices
1 tbsp. lemon juice

1. With a baller, cut the melon halves into balls and mix.
2. Sprinkle with lemon juice and put half into each of two stemmed cocktail glasses, or in bowls set in beds of crushed ice.

3. Garnish each cocktail with a slice of orange and refrigerate until time to serve.

Grilled Fillets of Flounder with Béarnaise Sauce

 2 *whole fillets flounder*
 2 *tbsp. olive oil*
 ½ *tsp. white pepper*

1. Heat your grill over high heat.
2. Wash and pat dry the flounder fillets.
3. Mix the pepper and the oil in a small bowl. Brush both sides of the fish with the mixture and also brush the ridges of the grill with it.
4. Grill the fillets for about 4 minutes on the first side, 3 on the second, turning only once. Use your largest spatula to turn the fish and do it very carefully to avoid breaking.
5. Serve hot with béarnaise sauce.

BEARNAISE SAUCE

Follow the directions for making hollandaise sauce in Lunch III, page 46, stirring in ½ teaspoon chopped parsley, ½ teaspoon tarragon, and 1 teaspoon tarragon vinegar at the very end.

Buttered Parsley Potatoes

Follow the directions for Boiled Parsley Potatoes in Dinner XI, page 129.

Steamed Cauliflower

1 small head cauliflower
2 tsp. salt
3 tbsp. breadcrumbs
2 tbsp. butter

1. Cut off the heavy stem of the cauliflower and break it up into florets.
2. Soak them in cold, salted water for about 30 minutes.
3. Remove from the water and steam over boiling water on a steaming platform for 12 minutes until tender.
4. While they are steaming, brown the breadcrumbs in the butter in a skillet.
5. Serve the cauliflower hot, with a generous spoonful of the butter and breadcrumb mixture alongside.

Fresh Mushroom and Lettuce Salad

1 small head bibb lettuce
6 large fresh mushrooms
3 strips bacon
2 tbsp. olive oil
1 tbsp. vinegar
½ tsp. salt
¼ tsp. pepper
1 tsp. Maggi seasoning

1. Fry the bacon until crisp, drain on paper towels, then crumble into the salad bowl. Then add the oil, vinegar, salt, pepper, and Maggi seasoning.
1. Wash and drain the lettuce, separating the leaves, and tearing them into 1½-inch pieces.
3. Clean the mushrooms with a damp cloth. Slice them

very thinly, stems and all, and put them in the bowl, then add the lettuce to the bowl.
4. Toss well and serve.

Sugared Strawberries and Cream

1 box fresh ripe strawberries
½ cup granulated sugar
1 tbsp. kirsch
½ pt. heavy cream, chilled
½ tsp. vanilla extract
2 tbsp. powdered (confectioners') sugar

1. Hull the strawberries, wash them under cold running water, and slice them into a bowl. Sprinkle them with the granulated sugar and the kirsch.
2. Put the chilled cream into a bowl with the vanilla extract. Beat until soft peaks are formed, then add the powdered sugar. Keep beating until it is well blended in.
3. Serve the strawberries on dessert plates, topped with the whipped cream.

~∿୨୧∿~

DINNER XXX
Stuffed Baked Oysters
Grilled Lamb Chops with Herb Butter
Sautéed Potato Balls
Green Goddess Salad
Coconut Gelatin with Raspberry Sauce
Red Wine
Coffee

~∿୨୧∿~

Stuffed Baked Oysters

1 doz. fresh oysters on the half shell
½ cup breadcrumbs
3 tbsp. butter
1 tbsp. chopped green peppers
1 tbsp. chopped onions
3 strips bacon, each cut into 4 pieces

1. Preheat oven to 375 degrees.
2. Melt the butter in a small skillet, sauté the onions and peppers in the melted butter over low heat. Stir in the breadcrumbs and blend thoroughly.
3. Set the oysters out on a cookie sheet or in a baking pan.
4. With a teaspoon, fill the oysters with the stuffing, dividing it as equally as possible among the oysters.
5. Top the stuffing in each oyster with 1 piece of bacon. Bake in middle level of preheated oven for 15 minutes until bacon browns.
6. Serve garnished with lemon wedges.

Grilled Lamb Chops with Herb Butter

4 tbsp. softened butter
1 tbsp. chopped fresh watercress
1 tbsp. chopped fresh parsley
1 tbsp. chopped fresh chives
¼ tsp. black pepper
4 loin lamb chops, about 1½ inches thick
1 tbsp. olive oil

1. In a bowl, blend together the herbs and butter thoroughly. Then pack into a small earthenware crock or other container and refrigerate.
2. Heat a stove-top grill over high heat and brush the raised ridges of the grill and the lamb chops on both sides with olive oil. Then rub both sides of the chops with the pepper.
3. Cook the chops about 5 minutes on each side.
4. When ready, transfer the chops to a warm serving platter and serve with the herb butter, which should be placed by the teaspoonful on top of each chop and allowed to melt on the plate.

Sautéed Potato Balls

3 large mature potatoes
1 tbsp. olive oil
1 tbsp. butter
1 tbsp. finely minced onion
¼ tsp. salt

1. Peel the potatoes, then cut into balls with a melon/potato baller.
2. Leave the potato balls in cold water until ready to cook. Drain on paper towel before cooking.

3. In a heavy iron skillet, heat the oil and butter until sizzling. Add onions and reduce heat. After about 30 seconds, add the potato balls and cook, turning frequently to brown all sides. You can check to see if they are sufficiently cooked by taking one ball out and cutting it open with a fork.

4. When ready, remove from pan with slotted spoon, place in serving dish, salt, and serve immediately, piping hot.

Green Goddess Salad

    1 head bibb lettuce
    1 head romaine lettuce
    1 tbsp. anchovy paste
    ¼ cup sour cream
    1 tbsp. chopped chives
    1 tsp. lemon juice
    1 tbsp. vinegar
    ¼ tsp. salt
    ¼ tsp. pepper
    1 small garlic clove

1. Wash lettuce thoroughly, tear, and place in colander to drain. Set aside.

2. Blend all remaining ingredients in blender until thoroughly combined.

3. Place lettuce in salad bowl, pour the dressing over, and toss until the leaves are well coated with the dressing. Toss the salad just before serving. Serve immediately.

Coconut Gelatin with Raspberry Sauce

For this recipe you need either two 1-cup individual molds or one 2-cup mold.

1 cup milk
1 cup cream of coconut concentrate (available canned)
5 drops almond extract
1 envelope unflavored gelatin
4 tbsp. sugar
1 tbsp. brandy
1 package frozen raspberries

1. Dissolve the gelatin powder in the milk, stirring until all the grains are absorbed. Place the milk in an enameled saucepan and stir in the coconut concentrate. Heat almost to the boiling point, but do not allow to boil. Now stir in the almond extract, sugar, and brandy. Warm another 2 minutes to melt the sugar, then remove from heat.
2. Pour the mixture into the mold(s) and refrigerate for several hours until gelatin is set. While gelatin is setting, thaw out the package of frozen raspberries.
3. To serve, unmold the gelatin onto serving plate or individual dessert plates. Spoon over thawed raspberries and serve.

Four Suppers for Two

❧❧❧❧❧❧❧❧❧❧❧❧❧❧❧❧❧❧❧❧❧❧❧❧❧❧

SUPPER I

Baked Virginia Ham with Madeira Gravy

Swiss Fondue

Egg and Potato Salad

Hot Chocolate with Cinnamon Sticks

❧❧❧❧❧❧❧❧❧❧❧❧❧❧❧❧❧❧❧❧❧❧❧❧❧❧

Baked Virginia Ham with Madeira Gravy

It is practically impossible to get a ham small enough to serve two people and allow them to finish it up in one sitting. However, I feel that in view of the excellence of cold, sliced ham, and the good use to which you can put a ham bone in making soups, it is permissible to recommend using this here. The cold, sliced ham may be used in several of the other recipes in this book.

½ cured Virginia ham, bone in
25 or 30 cloves
½ cup madeira wine

1. Trim the rind away from the ham, leaving an exposed layer of fat.
2. With a small sharp knife, score the exposed fat in a diamond pattern, cutting through almost to where the meat begins.
3. Insert 1 clove at each intersection of two knife scores, all over the fat side.
4. Bake the ham in a 350 degree oven for about 2 hours, basting occasionally with the drippings.
5. When ready, transfer ham to meat platter. Pour the madeira into the drippings in the baking pan. Hold the

pan over a medium heat and scrape the drippings into the gravy. Skim off about half the liquid fat, and pour what is left into the gravy boat to accompany the ham.

Swiss Fondue

½ lb. imported Swiss cheese
½ tsp. cornstarch
1 tbsp. brandy
1 cup dry white wine
½ tsp. salt
¼ tsp. cayenne pepper
toast or crusty french bread, cut into 2-inch pieces

1. To begin with, you must have some sort of heating utensil which can be used at the table. It can be a small electric hot plate or a chafing dish, or it may be a specially designed fondue pot.
2. In a cast iron or copper pot, bring the wine to a very gentle simmer over the lowest possible heat. While it is heating, run the cheese through the coarsest blade of your grater.
3. Stir the cheese into the hot wine, 1 tablespoon at a time, and allowing each addition to melt before adding the next. Keep stirring throughout this process.
4. Dissolve the cornstarch in the brandy, then stir it into the mixture.
5. Finally, add the salt and pepper and bring the pot to the table, placing it over the burner.
6. Serve the toast or bread with long forks to permit forking up a piece of toast, dipping in the fondue, and eating without getting burned!

Egg and Potato Salad

2 large mature potatoes
4 eggs
2 tsp. salt
1 tbsp. chopped parsley
1 tsp. white pepper
1 tbsp. olive oil
½ cup minced celery

1. Peel and boil the potatoes in water salted with 1 teaspoon salt.
2. When tender, but not too soft, remove the potatoes from the water and allow them to cool.
3. Hard-cook the eggs, peel, and let cool.
4. Cut the potatoes into small cubes, chop the eggs and put them both in a salad bowl along with all the other ingredients.
5. Toss lightly and refrigerate until serving time.

Hot Chocolate with Cinnamon Sticks

4 tbsp. Dutch or Swiss cocoa powder
4 tbsp. sugar
3 cups milk
boiling water
½ tsp. nutmeg
2 cinnamon sticks (at your grocer's on the spice rack)

1. In an enameled saucepan, mix together the sugar and the cocoa.
2. Add a little boiling water (about ¼ cup) and stir with a wooden spoon until the powder and the sugar have dissolved into a thick syrup. Turn heat on under the pan during this operation, if necessary.

3. Now stir in the milk and cook over medium heat until just short of the boiling point. Stir in the nutmeg.

4. When ready, serve in mugs with cinnamon sticks.

SUPPER II

Chicken Salad

Hot Biscuits with Honey

Fresh Fruit Compote

Iced Coffee

Chicken Salad

2 cups diced cooked chicken
2 hard-cooked eggs, chopped
1 medium-sized cucumber, peeled and diced
½ cup chopped celery
2 apples, peeled, cored, and diced
2 medium-sized potatoes, peeled and boiled, cut into cubes
½ cup mayonnaise
2 tbsp. lemon juice
1 tsp. Lawry's Seasoned Salt
½ tsp. freshly ground pepper
1 tsp. Maggi seasoning

1. In a large bowl combine all the ingredients in the order listed. Then toss thoroughly to spread the dressing evenly throughout.

2. Serve in individual salad bowls, on beds of lettuce leaves if you desire.

Hot Biscuits with Honey

1 cup sifted flour
½ tsp. baking soda
½ tsp. baking powder
½ tsp. salt
½ cup sour cream
honey

1. Sift the first four ingredients together into a bowl.
2. Preheat oven to 450 degrees.
3. Add the sour cream to the flour and stir. Knead to achieve a fairly soft dough.
4. Roll out on lightly floured board, about ¾ inch thick, then cut with round biscuit cutter.
5. Place the cut biscuits on a cookie sheet and bake for 15 minutes until light golden brown.
6. Serve hot with butter and honey.

Fresh Fruit Compote

The contents of this dessert should depend on the season and what's available at your market or fruit and vegetable dealer. The main point is to have at least six different kinds of fruit, and pieces that fit comfortably on a dessert spoon. Cut grapes in half; slice bananas not more than ¼ inch thick; use a melon baller for all melons; quarter, core, and slice the apples, pears, and similar fruits. Use a combination of fruit which looks attractive; for instance, combine bright red strawberries, green seedless grapes, pink melon, and white pears. Use enough fruit to make about four cups in all. Sprinkle generously with granulated sugar and about ¼ cup of kirsch. Toss lightly. Refrigerate for a few hours to chill well before serving.

SUPPER III

Hot Waffles with Raspberry Syrup
Grilled Sweet Italian Sausages
Cucumber Salad
Coffee

Hot Waffles with Raspberry Syrup

½ cup flour
2 tsp. baking powder
¼ tsp. salt
1 tsp. sugar
2 eggs, separated
½ cup heavy cream
raspberry syrup
½ cup melted butter

1. Sift the flour, sugar, and salt together into a mixing bowl.
2. In another bowl, beat the egg yolks and the cream together thoroughly, then beat in the dry ingredients.
3. Separately, beat the egg whites until they form soft peaks, then fold them into the mixture. Refrigerate while the waffle iron is heating.
4. Preheat the waffle iron, and follow the directions for baking the waffles. Most waffle irons have a thermostat which signals you when the waffles are ready, but you can tell when the edges, which puff out of the sides of the iron a little, start getting golden brown. At that point, lift the top half of the waffle iron very gently. If it opens

easily and the waffle doesn't stick, it is ready. If there is resistance to a gentle upward pressure, release the waffle and let bake longer.

5. Place a bottle of raspberry syrup in simmering water to heat. By the time the waffles are cooked, have the melted butter and syrup ready. Wipe off warm syrup bottle and bring syrup and butter to the table.

Grilled Sweet Italian Sausages

There are no complications to preparing these wonderful sausages. The main point is to get the right ones from the butcher. They are about 5 inches long, almost an inch in diameter, and a brownish-white color. Grill them on a stove-top grill or pan broil them in a heavy skillet. Two per person is plenty.

Cucumber Salad

2 medium-sized cucumbers
1 small jar pickled button mushrooms packed in olive oil
¼ tsp. black pepper
1 tbsp. vinegar

1. Peel the cucumbers, then run them through the slicing blade of your grater to get very thin slices.
2. Pour the liquid from the jar of mushrooms into a bowl, add the vinegar and the pepper and mix well.
3. Add the mushrooms and the sliced cucumbers to the bowl, toss, and serve.

SUPPER IV

Antipasto

Fettucine Alfredo

Meatballs in Sugo di Carne

Spumoni

Café Espresso

Antipasto

The assembling of an antipasto is primarily dependent on getting the proper ingredients and arranging them attractively rather than on cooking. Other ingredients may be substituted for those below, according to your own taste or preference, or that of your guest.

6 (or more) slices good Genoa salami
6 boned anchovy fillets
6 sardines, skinless and boneless
6 (or more) paper-thin slices of real prosciutto
1 cantaloupe, peeled, seeded, and cut into bite-sized wedges
6 hard-cooked egg halves
1 cup fresh crabmeat
mayonnaise (for crabmeat)
6 medium-sized mushroom caps, marinated in olive oil and vinegar for several hours

Arrange all the elements of the antipasto on a large platter in an attractive pattern, using a small bowl for the mayonnaise. Accompany with oil and vinegar, salt, and a pepper mill. Provide separate salad plates and serving spoons, and a fish knife and fork for each place setting.

Fettucine Alfredo

2 cups ½-inch-wide egg noodles
½ tsp. salt
4 tbsp. butter
1 egg
½ cup cream (or half-and-half)
½ cup grated fresh Parmesan cheese
½ tsp. freshly ground black pepper

1. Bring 3 quarts of water, with the salt added, to a full boil in a saucepan.
2. Throw in the noodles and boil for exactly 8 minutes, then remove from heat and pour into a colander to drain.
3. Melt the butter over low heat in a medium-sized enamel skillet. As soon as the butter is melted (do not let it brown), add the drained noodles to the skillet, then stir in the cream.
4. Beat the egg separately in a small bowl, then stir the beaten egg into the noodles. Add the grated Parmesan by sprinkling it over the surface of the noodles and stirring. Cover the skillet and allow the noodles to heat through without boiling.
5. Just before serving, sprinkle with the black pepper. Serve on warm plates after the antipasto has been cleared away.

Meatballs in Sugo di Carne

1 *lb. freshly ground round steak*
2 *tbsp. flour*
½ *cup finely chopped mushrooms*
¼ *cup finely chopped onions*
2 *tbsp. tomato paste*
1 *cup beef broth*
1 *tsp. salt*
½ *tsp. black pepper*

1. By hand, roll the ground beef into balls about 1 inch in diameter.
2. In a cast iron skillet, heat the olive oil over medium heat. Dust the meatballs with flour and brown them in the hot oil on all sides for about 5 minutes. Reduce heat to low.
3. Add the chopped mushrooms and onions to the pan and simmer for 2 or 3 minutes. Then add the tomato paste and the beef broth. Season with the salt and pepper and allow the contents of the skillet to simmer gently for 15 minutes.
4. Keep hot until ready to serve with the fettucine.

Spumoni

LIGHT PORTION

2 *egg yolks*
1 *tbsp. water*
2 *tbsp. sugar*
¼ *cup marsala wine (or any other sweet, white wine)*
½ *cup heavy cream*

1. Beat the egg yolks with the water, sugar, and wine.

Then transfer to a double boiler, and continue beating over simmering water until the mixture thickens. Remove from heat.

2. While the mixture is cooling, beat the heavy cream with an electric or hand beater until it forms stiff peaks.

3. When egg yolk mixture is cool, fold in whipped cream and transfer to ice cube tray, and place in freezer.

CHOCOLATE PORTION

3 tbsp. sugar
1 egg
1 tsp. flour
¼ cup milk
1 oz. melted semi-sweet chocolate
½ cup heavy cream

4. While the first part is freezing, prepare the chocolate portion. Mix the first 4 ingredients together and beat well. Then add the melted chocolate and stir.

5. Beat the heavy cream until stiff.

6. Fold the whipped cream into the chocolate mixture and cool. When the first portion is frozen solid, pour the chocolate on top of it and return to the freezer.

7. To serve, dip the tray into hot water for a few seconds to loosen. Reverse tray onto serving dish, and slice the spumoni.

Index

Page numbers in italics indicate menus.